TOXIC RELATIONSHIPS: BREATHE AGAIN

5 STEPS TO HEALING & RECOVERY; LETTING GO
AFTER LEAVING A NARCISSISTIC & EMOTIONALLY
ABUSIVE PARTNER TO REGAIN YOUR FREEDOM

LISANNE MURPHY

D1713557

Copyright © 2023 by Lisanne Murphy. All rights reserved.

The content contained within this book may not be reproduced, duplicated, or transmitted without direct written permission from the author or the publisher.

Under no circumstances will any blame or legal responsibility be held against the publisher, or author, for any damages, reparation, or monetary loss due to the information contained within this book, either directly or indirectly.

Legal Notice:

This book is copyright protected. It is only for personal use. You cannot amend, distribute, sell, use, quote, or paraphrase any part, or the content within this book, without the consent of the author or publisher.

Disclaimer Notice:

Please note the information contained within this document is for educational and entertainment purposes only. All effort has been executed to present accurate, up-to-date, reliable, and complete information. No warranties of any kind are declared or implied. Readers acknowledge that the author is not engaged in the rendering of legal, financial, medical, or professional advice. The content within this book has been derived from various sources. Please consult a licensed professional before attempting any techniques outlined in this book.

By reading this document, the reader agrees that under no circumstances is the author responsible for any losses, direct or indirect, that are incurred as a result of the use of the information contained within this document, including, but not limited to, errors, omissions, or inaccuracies.

CONTENTS

INTRODUCTION

> ❝ *"No partner in a love relationship... should feel that he(she) has to give up an essential part of himself(herself) to make it viable."*
>
> — MAY SARTON

As I sat across from my friend Lily in a bustling coffee shop, I couldn't help but notice the sadness in her voice as she talked about her traumatic relationship with her ex-boyfriend, Jack. It was the first time Lily confided in me about the toxic dynamics she experienced. As her friend and colleague, I was amazed to see how much she suffered.

As I listened, I realized how prevalent toxic relationships are in our society and how many people are stuck in them without knowing how to break free, even after the breakup. If you're in a similar situation, feeling trapped in pain and guilt, and unsure how to move forward, this book is for you.

For most, the mental and emotional attachment to a toxic partner can continue long after the relationship has ended. Understandably, you may feel overwhelmed and struggle with the emotional baggage left behind, no matter how much time has passed. After all, toxic people know how to undermine your confidence and leave you feeling heartbroken and unsure of what you want or need to heal to make the most of your life. The pain can sometimes be intense and overwhelming, and its crippling nature can hold you back from reaching your full potential or simply being happy again.

Even if you've broken free successfully, there may be fear of trusting in love again. If you missed the red flags in the past, what would stop you from falling in love with someone toxic in the future? This feeling, combined with the emotional wounds left by this traumatic experience, leaves a feeling of powerlessness, without a clear picture of who we are, and unable to see the silver lining in our circumstances.

The fear of being hurt again can be paralyzing, and the thought of repeating the same cycle can be terrifying. However, it is possible to heal and break free from the cycle of toxic relationships. Creating and enjoying healthy and fulfilling connections in your life is not something that only happens in the movies. The important truth is turning your gaze inward and learning the 5 practical steps to help yourself heal from the abuse you've just experienced.

For my friend, Lily, the longing for closure and wanting to put the relationship behind was pressing. Lily sometimes felt guilty or inadequate for not feeling like the person she was before she met Jack. But she would never be the same because this relationship triggered a powerful healing process that unlocked her inner potential.

By reading this book, you'll gain valuable insights and practical strategies to help you on your journey of healing and growth. First, you'll understand exactly how you ended up in a toxic relationship, and most importantly, what your role was in the toxic relationship. (I know this notion can sound crazy, but just hang with me.) Examining the patterns and behaviors that led to toxicity is key to creating closure, healing from the trauma you've experienced, and not repeating the cycle.

Another important step to learning to move on from a toxic relationship is to go through the pain you are experiencing. There's no other way than to embrace it and allow yourself to grieve the relationship and the person you were in it. This book offers guidance and meaningful strategies for befriending that pain instead of making it an enemy.

After connecting with your emotions, you can work on your self-esteem and take a more compassionate approach to your suffering. As you see yourself through understanding eyes, you'll realize the importance of asking for help and leaning on your support network. This experience will help you rebuild your identity and rediscover the values and interests lost during your toxic relationship.

This book will also help you create firm boundaries to protect this newfound identity and be better equipped to avoid falling back into a toxic cycle. This will create a foundation for healthy relationships moving forward.

With the insights and guidance offered in this book, you can let go of self-blame and forgive yourself for what happened. You can release guilt and move toward greater self-compassion and forgiveness–the foundations of a healthy and powerful existence.

I've also had my share of toxic relationships with bosses, friends, and family. I spent too long trying unsuccessful methods, reading self-help books, and following anecdotal advice from friends and the internet. But the pain and suffering simply didn't go away. I was repeatedly hurt, and those hurts accumulated in my mind and body. I started to live a jaded life where I struggled to trust anyone. The fears of my past overshadowed my present. I lost my confidence, questioned my intuition, and didn't know who I was or what I wanted. I was a wreck. That's why I decided to make a 180-degree turn and go to a monastery in France to live like a monk. Live a simple, ascetic life devoted to spiritual practice and contemplation to understand and take care of the root causes of my suffering.

The lessons I learned allowed me to find healing and clarity from the emotional baggage I carried from these toxic relationships. I realized that the path to healing is simple yet counterintuitive. However, it requires a firm commitment and a burning desire to be vulnerable and look at yourself clearly to rediscover self-identity. Not only did I live at the monastery for a time, but I also engaged in multiple kinds of formal therapy, such as talk therapy and EMDR. I also hired a life coach to help my process and engaged daily in meditation, journal writing, and exercise to regain my balance. I threw everything I could get my hands on at the proverbial trauma wall created by my multiple encounters with toxic people.

My recovery from my traumas inspired me to reach out to people in the same situation as Lily and me. I want to help others see a way out of pain and suffering and regain control of life without uprooting everything and flying around the world as I did.

Whether you have just left a toxic relationship or are still struggling with the emotional aftermath, this book is designed to help you move into a healthy and meaningful life without being so hard on yourself and repeating missteps of the past. Using The 5 Steps to Healing and Recovery, you can live your true potential of having a joyful and fulfilling relationship with yourself and others. You have already started on the path, now let's make it stick.

1

UNRAVELING THE COMPLEXITIES OF A TOXIC RELATIONSHIP

> *"Love should not make you feel like walking on eggshells."*
>
> — EMMA XU

Lily's whole world fell apart at that moment. You know that moment when you feel your heart drop into your stomach and the same adrenaline rush from a near-miss car accident; because your worst fear just became a potential reality? Yeah, that's what it was like for Lily. Jack walked in and found her crying on the floor. Lily, angry and devastated, confronted him about the messages on his Skype account. His face twisted into a sneer as he denied wrongdoing and yelled at her for suggesting it.

Toxic relationships never begin as toxic, but rather the opposite. Most toxic relationship stories, like my friend Lily's, begin like a fairy tale, full of passion, excitement, and love. Lily's partner seemed to complement her, seeing what no one else saw in her. She felt like he knew exactly what was going on in her mind–it was a rush unlike anything she had ever felt before.

According to the study by Günnur Karakurt, Ph.D and Kristin E. Silver, B. A., nearly half of all women (48.4%) and men (48.8%) have experienced some form of psychological aggression (toxicity) from a partner. Statistics like these indicate that relationship aggression from a partner is much more common than the few sensational stories showcased on shows like Jerry Springer. The numbers are not only high, but what's more alarming is most people in toxic relationships don't know how or why they got there. For this reason, understanding what a toxic relationship is and is not is essential in identifying if you are in a toxic relationship and addressing the situation.

To do this, let's return to the beginning of the story we introduced earlier. This friend helped me realize the reality and prevalence of toxic relationships, even the hidden ones in my own life. Her vulnerable story, filled with the wounds of narcissism and gaslighting (which, at the time of initially hearing her story, were foreign concepts to me), is shared with her permission, and the names are changed.

Lily was never the outgoing, bubbly, rebellious type of girl. I met her at one of my part-time jobs while I was finishing school, and we clicked right away thanks to her sweet and understanding nature. Lily was always early, did her work perfectly, got good grades, had a few close friends, wouldn't say bad things about anyone, and mostly stayed under the radar. That's why her story with Jack hit me like a ton of bricks. It started great, like all love stories…

Jack seemed to be the perfect partner. Confident, charming, eloquent, and attractive. He exuded the traits of a natural leader who knew exactly what he wanted in life. His charisma and self-assuredness captivated Lily. She felt incredibly lucky when he asked her out.

The first several months of the relationship were like a dream come true. They quickly went from seeing each other on weekends to every day. It wasn't long before they could never get enough of each other. Jack was Lily's first thought every day. From the moment Lily opened her eyes, she sent him a good morning text, and he immediately responded with passionate, almost poetic replies.

Then Jack regularly arrived at Lily's work with a gift: a bouquet of seasonal flowers, her favorite cookie of the month, creatively folded love letters...you name it! Jack's attention exhilarated her. She almost felt like she was floating rather than walking. Jack's care also got Lily the attention of her co-workers, who envied Jack's adoration of her. She told me how good that felt too. Her world was expanding in a beautiful way. For all of this, Lily gave Jack unlimited, unconditional devotion.

But, like every fairy tale, conflict arises. Like Snow White biting the poisoned apple or Sleeping Beauty pricking her finger on the spindle, it became clear that this story was riddled with a dark side.

After Lily and Jack moved in together, things began to change. Jack's charm and wit transformed into demands, criticism, and emotional distance. Lily constantly tried to please him, going to great lengths to make him happy and sacrificing her needs and desires.

Jack would punish her with a cold demeanor that deeply disturbed her whenever she failed to praise his decisions or actions. She always seemed to be apologizing for making him upset. To maintain the relationship, she would prepare his favorite meal, cancel appointments with friends and coworkers to be there for him, and agree to his travel plans, even if it meant neglecting her work and personal responsibilities.

At the beginning of the relationship, Jack made her feel like the God of Olympus had chosen her from millions of mortals. Therefore, her mission in life was to make Jack happy. She didn't want him to wake up one day and find himself thinking he was actually out of her league.

One morning, while Lily was busy trying to prepare herself and Jack for success by meal prepping and getting ready for the day, she heard the familiar *bing* of a message notification. Jack's laptop was open while he was in the shower, and messages started coming in on his Skype account. In an act of impulsivity, Lily clicked on a conversation with a coworker she had never heard of, telling him what a great time she had at dinner with him the night before. Jack walked in and found Lily crying on the floor. Lily, angry and devastated, confronted him about the messages on his Skype account.

Despite the evidence staring him in the face, Jack completely denied what was happening. In fact, his face twisted into a sneer as he denied any wrongdoing and yelled at her for suggesting it. He told her she was being sensitive and was looking for excuses to ruin the relationship because SHE was unhappy.

Whenever Lily tried to bring up the incident again, Jack would get angry and leave the house, turn off his phone, and leave her in fear, anxiety, worry, and pain. He kept telling her she was emotionally unstable and that she remembered things differently than they actually happened. Lily felt confused and ashamed, leading her to believe she could not confide in anyone about what was happening.

As a result, she began to doubt her memories, and what little self-confidence she had left– collapsed. She was constantly anxious, emotionally exhausted, and confused. She even blamed herself for Jack's emotional distance. Remember, she was the one who was lucky to be with him, right?

Lily made every decision and action to keep Jack by her side, thinking that if she could just be with him more, he wouldn't have the need or time to message anyone else. It wasn't long before Lily lost touch with all her friends, no longer spoke to her coworkers outside of work-related matters, and rarely visited her family. Lily became a shadow of her former self, consumed by her fear that Jack would leave her.

She built her entire life around avoiding making Jack unhappy, which seemed impossible. On the one hand, she felt he loathed her, and on the other, he seemed to need her praise with every decision, action, and accomplishment.

Jack spent more and more time away from home and sometimes even stayed out all night. When Lily dared to confront him, his rage took over, and he punished her with contempt and alienation, somehow making it Lily's fault.

When Lily hit rock bottom, she stopped communicating with her family. Her sister came to check in and observe what was wrong and could see Lily had lost herself completely in Jack. Lily couldn't recognize the situation clearly. With great convincing, her sister helped Lily pack her things and, with her last shreds of strength, left the house.

By this point in Lily's story, I couldn't stop the tears from rolling down my cheeks. Lily said it took her a long time to accept that she was in a toxic relationship. She was sure she was to blame for the failure of her relationship, and it was only after a long journey of therapy, deep conversations with other toxic relationship victims, and personal reflection that she understood what happened to her "once upon a time" fairy tale story.

Her story deeply moved me, and I saw myself in many of her experiences. I had never heard of narcissism or gaslighting. But hearing her story struck a chord in my heart that motivated me to investigate more about toxic relationships, which now brings me here with you.

- Why did this relationship turn from a fairy tale to a horror story?
- How did Lily miss that she had been in a toxic relationship for so long?
- What makes this a toxic relationship from a psychological perspective?
- Was Jack a narcissist?
- What role did gaslighting play in Lily isolating herself from her world outside Jack and not seeing the problems for so long?

Understanding these concepts is essential to recognizing toxic behavior in our relationships and taking steps to address it.

WAS YOUR RELATIONSHIP TOXIC?

Simply put, a toxic relationship makes you feel worse, not better, over time. Remember how Lily's happiness, attention, and near infatuation turned to anxiety, depression, and guilt as the relationship progressed? She even felt like she couldn't focus on any other relationship but hers and Jack's. She also felt misunderstood or unsupported and, sometimes worse, attacked or threatened. Lily couldn't communicate her feelings and needs safely with Jack or anyone else (so she thought) without being ridiculed. (1)

No relationship is all butterflies and roses. Acknowledging and resolving conflict is a natural and healthy aspect of bringing lives together in a partnership. However, if the scales are tipped consistently, it's time to determine if the relationship brings more stress and suffering than ease and happiness into your life.

It's also important to note that toxic relationships can occur in any context: romantic, professional, with friends, or with family. While most of this book is focused on toxic romantic relationships, the principles and lessons gained apply to all types of relationships. It is also important to note that while this book centers around a heterosexual relationship, correlations and similarities can be drawn to any other type of romantic relationship.

As a special bonus, exclusively for readers of this book, there is an additional chapter that delves deeper into toxic relationships at work and among family and friends. Go to www.healingtoxicity.com/breathe-again-bonus for this free Ebook.

The signs of a toxic relationship can be subtle. Verbal or physical violence is not the only sign of toxicity in a relationship.

- You give more than the other person gives.
- The other person never respects your boundaries or meets your needs.
- Your self-esteem diminishes.
- You feel anxious, tired, or depressed after spending time with this person.
- You bring out the worst qualities in each other.
- You are not your best self around this person.
- Everything you say or do triggers the other person, making you feel like you are walking on eggshells.
- It takes a lot of emotional effort to cheer this person up.
- They blame you for all their problems.

How many of the above signs were present in your last relationship? Chances are high your relationship is/was toxic if you find yourself nodding your head or saying yes to several of these points. (1)

DISCERNING BETWEEN HEALTHY & UNHEALTHY BEHAVIORS

When lost in a toxic relationship, "love" tends to muddy the distinction between healthy and unhealthy behaviors. Seeing them side by side helps regain clarity. Take a look at which ones are more common in your interactions. These parameters can help you determine the toxicity of a relationship.

Toxic behaviors may come from you or your partner. The key is recognizing and addressing them quickly, regardless of source, so they do not become patterns. (1)

Toxic Behavior	Healthy Behavior
Self-doubting	Confident
Possessive	Loving
Discouraging	Supportive
Self-centered	Giving
Inconsiderate	Considerate
Judgmental	Tolerant
Belittling	Praising
Suspicious	Trustworthy
Abusive	Kind
Rude	Respectful

Jack was self-centered and insensitive to Lily's needs and feelings. He never showed interest in Lily's values, goals, and passions, nor did he give his time or attention to support her aspirations. Jack always discouraged her from pursuing activities alone or even going out with her friends and family, which are clear examples of unhealthy toxic behavior.

At the same time, Lily struggled with self-doubt, especially when Jack dismissed her concerns or requests. She became overly dependent on his validation and reassurance instead of feeling confident to take action without Jack's input or support. This behavior made it easy for him to be rude and abusive throughout the relationship, thus perpetuating the unhealthy toxic cycle.

Two critical components in Jack and Lily's story made the relationship toxic: narcissism and gaslighting.

RECOGNIZING NARCISSISTIC & GASLIGHTING TENDENCIES

If you've gotten this far, you've probably confirmed your relationship was toxic in some or many ways. Patterns of narcissism and gaslighting are often traits of toxic relationships. They create a codependent mess of confusion and a feeling of being stuck in a loveless yet addictive relationship.

Identifying and naming these toxic elements is a powerful source of clarity that brings awareness and healing.

Narcissism

Narcissism is a personality trait characterized by excessive self-love, self-absorption, and an inflated sense of self-importance. People with narcissistic traits have a deep need for admiration and attention and may be preoccupied with fantasies of power, success, and attractiveness.

You've probably heard of Narcissistic Personality Disorder (NPD), a specific psychiatric diagnosis characterized by a pervasive pattern of grandiosity, a need for admiration, and a lack of empathy. (2)

Approximately 1 in 200 people, or 0.5% of the USA population, has this personality disorder. But while some people with narcissistic traits may exhibit some of the behaviors associated with NPD, not all individuals with narcissistic traits meet the diagnostic criteria for NPD. (3)

In popular culture, narcissism is associated with people who love themselves to the point of subconscious obsession. Yet, this personality trait has nothing to do with self-love. Narcissistic people have an idealized view of themselves. These individuals perceive themselves as thriving, strong, ultra-confident, and powerful. This image acts as a carcass that protects them from dealing with their deep feelings of self-doubt and insecurity.

Jack felt superior to the world around him. He needed others to constantly remind him of his superiority through an insatiable thirst for attention and praise, which came easily from Lily.

Jack also had a sense of entitlement and expected others to recognize and fulfill his needs and desires. At the same time, he disregarded the feelings and opinions of others as if they were insignificant compared to his superior intellect.

Another significant characteristic of narcissists is that they cannot handle feedback or criticism. Jack always became defensive or aggressive when he felt his sense of self was challenged, so Lily learned to keep her opinions to herself to avoid conflict.

Healthy relationships are based on a sense of balance and harmony. However, narcissists are not interested in anything outside their needs and desires. This is why Jack never asked Lily how she felt or what she wanted throughout their relationship. It was all about fulfilling his desires and him feeling insulted when they were not met.

This led to a toxic dynamic in which Lily was constantly giving while Jack only took, yet neither party was ever fully satisfied.

Gaslighting

Gaslighting refers to actions, tactics, and behaviors intentionally designed to manipulate others into questioning their sanity. Whether consciously or subconsciously, the gaslighter aims to make you doubt your memories, experiences, and reality. (4)

According to YouGov research, 75% of US adults have never heard the term "gaslighting" before, which makes it challenging to identify. (5)

This type of manipulation is born out of someone's desperate need to be right, regardless of whether it hurts someone else. Remember how Jack denied cheating on Lily even when the evidence was right in front of him? That is precisely what gaslighting looks like.

Jack was determined to maintain his version of the story until Lily believed him, even if it made her feel insecure, hurt, and confused. Of course, this is not the typical behavior we expect from people, especially our romantic partners. After all, Jack was telling her to her face that what he was saying was true. For this reason, Lily felt she had no choice but to believe him, even though it went against her memories, evidence, and intuition.

Examples of Gaslighting:

Use the examples below of gaslight types to see if you've experienced this manipulative tactic.

Countering is when the gaslighter questions your memories and past experiences. They accomplish this by saying things like "Your memory is failing" or asking questions like "Are you sure that's what happened?"

Withholding involves acting as if they don't understand what you're saying or aren't paying attention. The goal is to make you doubt your coherence by saying things like, "You're confusing me" or "I don't know what you're talking about."

Trivializing is the classic "you're overreacting" or "you're being too sensitive" response to your legitimate concerns. Jack's favorite. The purpose of this tactic is to disregard your opinions and feelings.

Denying includes blaming others for the negative consequences of their choices. Most gaslighters with NPD refuse to take responsibility for their actions. Therefore, they deny that they ever did them in the first place.

Diverting is when the gaslighter changes the focus of attention. Instead of discussing your concerns, they question your credibility. A classic example is when they say, "That's just nonsense. It's not real," when you express your concerns.

Stereotyping is when the gaslighter uses negative stereotypes about your race, gender, nationality, ethnicity, or the like to manipulate you. (4)

HOW GASLIGHTING & NARCISSISM ARE RELATED

Now, with a brief introduction about narcissism and gaslighting, I'm sure you can start to estimate how many times in your life you've encountered someone with these traits using these techniques. And as you can see, the two are closely related.

Narcissists use gaslighting as a manipulation technique to feed their sense of grandeur. It allows them to maintain their lies even when the evidence is against them. They don't want others to see that underneath their shiny, attractive mask is a bundle of insecurities.

Knowing when your partner is gaslighting you can be difficult. Recognizing the signs is vital to taking action. (6)

Signs Someone with Narcissistic Tendencies is Gaslighting You

Do you suspect you are a victim of this type of manipulation? Look at these signs to determine if you've been a victim of gaslighting:

- Constantly questioning your decisions.
- Constantly wondering if you are overreacting to things.
- Feeling emotionally unstable or like you are losing your mind.
- You are constantly apologizing to the other person.
- You feel unhappier with each passing day.

Recognizing the signs of gaslighting can help protect yourself from being manipulated by your romantic partner and anyone else you meet.

The Corrosive Effects of Toxic Relationships On Your Health

Toxic relationships can slowly erode your self-esteem, confidence, and overall well-being. Being in a constant state of flight or fight increases stress levels. As a result, you may suffer from insomnia, depression, anxiety, and other similar symptoms. (1)

These toxic relationships consume a lot of time and emotional energy, alienating us from other relationships and activities. Lily shut down her world to be with Jack, which inevitably led to depression and anxiety symptoms, and over time her mental health deteriorated. (1)

Lily's story highlights her toxic relationship with Jack. However, through her healing journey, she later discovered that her relationship with her parents wasn't particularly healthy, nor was her association with her former boss. Toxicity rarely begins in a romantic relationship that becomes toxic. Understanding this is key to healing and not repeating the toxic cycle in future relationships, which will be the focus of the next chapter. Any toxic relationship can affect your overall well-being, especially if not understood and managed effectively.

MAKE IT STICK

Instructions: Take some time to reflect on the prompts and responses below to assess the toxicity of your relationship. Answer each question honestly and thoughtfully.

As you read about Lily and Jack, did you see yourself and the elements of your relationship in Lily and Jack's relationship story? *Answer Yes or No. Also, elaborate on your experience in the space provided.*

_____

_____

_____

_____

_____

Did you feel constantly anxious, depressed, or drained in your relationship? *Answer Yes or No. Also, elaborate on your experience in the space provided.*

_____

_____

_____

_____

_____

Did your partner frequently criticize, belittle, or insult you privately or in public? *Answer Yes or No. Also, elaborate on your experience in the space provided.*

_____

_____

_____

_____

_____

Did your partner try to control or manipulate you by withholding affection, finances, or decision-making power? *Answer Yes or No. Also, elaborate on your experience in the space provided.*

_____

_____

_____

_____

_____

Did your partner frequently engage in angry outbursts, emotional abuse, or physical violence toward you? *Answer Yes or No. Also, elaborate on your experience in the space provided.*

_____

_____

_____

_____

_____

Did you feel like your needs, feelings, and boundaries were consistently ignored or dismissed by your partner? *Answer Yes or No. Also, elaborate on your experience in the space provided.*

_____

_____

_____

_____

_____

Scoring: Give yourself 1 point for every "yes" answer. If you score 3 or more may indicate you were in a toxic relationship.

Remember, it is not your fault you were in a toxic relationship. You deserve to be treated with respect and love in all your relationships. Writing about your experiences is a powerful tool for clarity and healing.

2

HOW DID I GET HERE? UNDERSTANDING YOUR ROLE IN A TOXIC RELATIONSHIP

66 *"We are taught you must blame your father, your sisters, your brothers, the school, the teachers - but never blame yourself. It's never your fault. But it's always your fault because if you want to change, you're the one who has got to change."*

— KATHARINE HEPBURN

Jack was Lily's first real relationship, so the truth is, she could not have known better when she entered her soon-to-become toxic relationship. However, certain elements of her background may give us clues as to how Lily became attracted to a narcissistic partner like Jack.

Lily was accustomed to taking care of everyone else's wants and needs. Her parents, good middle-class Catholics, always told her that putting her desires first was selfish and that passion or anger were negative emotions to be swept under the rug.

She grew up as a shy and obedient child and later as a teenager who got good grades, did her chores, and tried not to bother the people around her. She was conditioned to believe that expressing her desires was shameful and that her role as a "good girl" was to please others.

At the same time, she always thought of herself as a selfless girl who would go out of her way to help those around her. Lily would give her lunch to the first hungry person she met on the street, even if it meant starving herself until the next meal. This selflessness was a badge of honor that became a part of her identity.

Her urge to make other people happy resulted in her inability to set limits (known as boundaries) to protect her well-being. She was used to taking extra work home with her, staying late to help her classmates study, and sacrificing her free time to assist her parents with their business on weekends. Again, a badge of honor that strengthened this selfless, serve-to-the-extreme identity.

No wonder why Jack's initial interest quickly swept her off her feet. No one had ever paid as much attention to her as Jack. Lily, smitten, would stay up all night rereading the texts Jack sent her during the day. She became head over heels in love with his quick wit, sharp sense of humor, and his life story.

Jack had a rough childhood. His parents died in a car accident when he was just a baby, leaving him an orphan and bouncing from foster home to foster home until some distant relatives were able to adopt him. This story touched Lily deeply, and she decided to do everything she could to "make up for his loss" and make Jack happy. Her natural caretaker role created a sense of happiness and support for him.

Lily is not to blame for the suffering she experienced in her toxic relationship with Jack. However, understanding her role in the toxicity illuminates that this was not a simple matter of bad luck. Healing isn't about blame and fault. It's about shining a light on our automatic subconscious behaviors and taking charge of our blind spots so we don't repeat the same patterns in the future.

Lily's strong need to please and even save people from their problems and her low self-esteem and difficulty setting clear boundaries created a strong propensity towards codependency. Which, in turn, made her an easy target for a narcissist like Jack. Essentially Lily's wounds created a toxic cocktail with Jack's wounds.

- What was Lily's role in this toxic relationship?
- How do Lily's background and childhood wounds contribute to the toxic dynamic of her relationship?
- What can Lily do to avoid falling into the same toxic cycle in the future?
- What role did Lily's lack of self-esteem play in the relationship?
- Was Lily in love with Jack or emotionally dependent on him or both?

WHY DO YOU TEND TO ATTRACT TOXIC PARTNERS?

To summarize Lily's story, several key points made her "easy bait" for a narcissist like Jack. First and foremost was her compassionate nature, always willing to help others. This is called the "**savior mentality**," which led her to nurture Jack's inner emotional child. This mentality meant that Lily always conformed to his terms and only considered her needs as a secondary thought or not at all.

Next, we can see how Lily was **recreating her childhood** in her toxic relationship. Remember how her parents taught her that expressing her needs was selfish and shameful? She was raised to believe that needs were selfish. So, she didn't know any other way than to stuff her own needs and desires so as not to communicate selfishness. Dealing with our emotional baggage is essential to not recreating poor dynamics in future relationships.

Another personality trait that attracts narcissistic partners is a **constant need to please people**. Lily rarely said no to Jack's requests because she feared being disliked or rejected by him. At the same time, she was terrified of confrontation, so she avoided conflict and agreed with everything Jack said. Fear drove her actions of affection. This is not a healthy pattern in building a relationship.

Moreover, Lily was **radically loyal**. She was convinced that Jack would eventually change and that he was just going through a phase. As a result, Lily **never really set strong boundaries** and could not leave the relationship sooner. (1)

Do you identify with any of these behaviors? How often in your relationship have you avoided speaking up for fear of being rejected? How often have you wanted to "save" your partner, even at the expense of your well-being?

Please recognize that none of these traits are inherently "bad." Loyalty, service, and thinking of others are incredible attributes. However, an overabundance of them in combination creates a recipe for a codependent-based toxic relationship.

Now that we know what characteristics and personality traits contributed to Lily being easy bait for someone like Jack, let's look at why she had them in the first place. A lack of self-esteem and a negative family background often lead to codependency. Which gives key insights into the common question, "Why did you stay in the relationship for so long if you were so unhappy?

CODEPENDENCY: YOUR ROLE IN TOXICITY & WHY IT'S SO HARD TO LET GO

Emotional dependency, or codependency, is deriving personal happiness and psychological safety by prioritizing your partner's needs above your own. It manifests in a lack of boundaries and psychological reliance on your partner. We have numerous examples of how Lily depended on Jack for her sense of self-worth. She invested excessive time in her relationship with Jack, putting her other relationships, hobbies, and work on the back burner. (5)

Emotionally dependent people easily empathize with their partner's emotional needs and problems. This is not inherently a negative thing. However, codependency does not refer to our love and care for others, but rather when our identity and happiness are contingent on another person. The real problem with codependency is that the giver loses their sense of self to an unhealthy degree. (2)

Lily quickly sacrificed her needs and devoted all her time and energy to Jack's benefit without expecting similar behavior in return. Her wants and needs quickly took a back seat, which took a toll on her emotional and psychological well-being.

Being in a cycle of codependency is sneaky. If you knew you were in it, you would get out. But the keys to releasing the chains of codependency don't lie in the codependent relationship. The keys to unlocking codependent habits live internally. Uncovering the elements of Low self-esteem and core wounds formed during childhood are the keys to look for.

If we come from a negative and invalidating family background, it will seem normal to silence needs and sacrifice well-being so that we will not be abandoned. After all, if we don't have enough love and respect within ourselves, we depend on the person that gives us attention and affection to feel safe and not fall apart.

Fortunately, even though all of these behaviors were "learned" subconsciously, they can also be "unlearned" consciously once we understand where they come from.

FAMILY BACKGROUND: WHERE RELATIONSHIP PATTERNS ARE LEARNED. (THE REASON WHY YOUR TOXIC RELATIONSHIP IS NOT YOUR FAULT.)

Now, with an overview of codependency, it's time to take a step back and realize the problem goes back much further than the toxic relationship.

Early family experiences can affect our relationships later in life, especially romantic ones. Growing up in a dysfunctional family environment can shape how you approach reality and relationships. For example, you may have learned that it is normal for the person you love to ghost you, to be abusive, or to be indifferent to your desires. (3) (6)

Lily never saw her parents discuss their feelings. Her parents rarely spoke on a deep level with each other. She grew up believing it was normal for your desires never to be revealed to another. Keeping deep feelings inside seemed the way to a successful relationship.

They seemed like a nice family from the outside because they never argued or raised their voices. Anger and resentment were swept under the rug, and anything negative was ignored or denied, inadvertently creating an unhealthy dynamic.

How did you handle conflicts in your family? Were you able to openly express your feelings, even negative ones? How did your parents communicate with each other or express affection?

Effects of Family Patterns: Lack of Self-Esteem

What happens when your family never validates your feelings, encourages you to communicate your ideas, or helps you discover your uniqueness and creativity? Answer: A lack of self-esteem that manifests in toxic and codependent relationships.

People who struggle with **low self-esteem** are accustomed to getting caught up in **cycles of negative thought patterns and behaviors** without realizing it. These individuals tend to have a deep-seated core belief that they will never be successful, loved, or happy enough. Therefore, when they face challenges in different areas of their lives, the automatic thoughts that are triggered are "That's why no one loves me," or "I knew I'd screw up again," or "I'm ugly/dumb/useless."

In response to these thoughts, our brain accepts these negative thoughts as truths and translates them into personal beliefs. As a result, these poor beliefs dictate action or inaction. For example, if you truly believe that "you'll never find love," then you will act as if it's true. You will cling to anyone who gives you unlimited attention, no matter how healthy or unhealthy that attention may be. That's why they avoid taking risks to improve their situation or to set strong boundaries in their relationships.

People who struggle with low self-esteem **need the affection and validation of others** because they feel they can't get it on their own. That's why Lily relied on Jack's "love" or attention to make her feel worthy and could not assertively communicate her needs or concerns within the relationship. In essence, she lived out the belief that meeting his needs was meeting her needs.

A 2018 study in two groups of around 100 couples in the Personality and Social Psychology Bulletin found that people with low self-esteem tend to **seek support through sadness or whining** to protect themselves from rejection. Contrary to what they want, their partners tend to react negatively to these behaviors, undermining the need for the affection they desperately crave. (4)

Lily had never been able to **express her emotional needs assertively**. When her anxiety was overwhelming, she would wake up at night and cry incessantly, waiting for Jack to comfort her. The more she cried, the more Jack ignored her and the angrier he became! This led to more negative interactions that perpetuated the cycle of toxicity.

At the same time, people who struggle with low self-esteem fear being alone because **they can't find enough validation, love, and acceptance from within.** As a result, they stay in relationships that aren't good for their well-being because, deep down, they feel it's better than being alone. Little do they know that the criticism, rejection, and gaslighting they endure in the relationship hurt their self-esteem even more.

Because Lily engaged in this dangerous cycle where she could not give the love and respect she needed to herself, it was nearly impossible to break down her codependency to end the toxic relationship. The worst part is that most people in this same position think the toxicity is normal, especially women. After all, society encourages us to sacrifice ourselves to protect the feelings of others. Our society is riddled with a normalized sense of low self-esteem.

Effects of Family Patterns: Core Wounds

Core emotional wounds refer to deep-seated emotional injuries that often develop in childhood. They result from internalized experiences such as neglect, abuse, abandonment, or other traumatic events. As we grow up, these wounds can affect our emotional and psychological well-being, relationships, and overall quality of life. It's important to note that trauma is not what happens to us but what happens inside us. This is important because there doesn't need to be a catastrophic traumatic event to develop a trauma response that seeds a core wound. (8)

- **The shame wound:** If you were publicly shamed or embarrassed as a child, you might feel socially anxious or constantly ashamed of your actions, choices, or interactions. This wound is manifested in beliefs such as *"I am afraid to make mistakes, " "I am inherently flawed and defective," or "I feel like a failure because I can't seem to get anything right."*
- **The judgment wound:** This core emotional wound occurs after you have been harshly judged and criticized in your childhood. This wound is manifested in beliefs such as *"I feel like everyone else is doing better than me," or "I am not*

as good as others," or "I feel like I can't be myself in front of others."

- **The betrayal wound:** If you could not rely on your parents or caregivers in your childhood, you may be afraid to open up to others because they may hurt or leave you, as others did in the past. This wound is manifested in beliefs such as *"I am unable to trust anyone," or "I feel like I'm always waiting for the other shoe to drop," or "I feel like anyone I care about will eventually hurt me."*

- **The rejection wound:** If you experienced rejection as a child, you might believe you are not good enough in adult relationships. You may struggle with low self-esteem and a fear of failure and constantly seek validation and approval from others. This wound is manifested in beliefs such as *"I feel like I will never measure up to other people's expectations," or "I am unworthy of love or attention," or "I feel like I always need to be perfect and meet others to avoid rejection."*

- **The abandonment wound:** This emotional wound occurs when your parents or caregivers abandoned you in childhood. This experience may cause you to cling to people because you fear they will also leave you. This wound is manifested in beliefs such as *"I am afraid people*

*will leave me," or "I am convinced people will always
leave me, so I don't even bother getting close to
anyone," or "I am afraid to trust others." or "My
needs are not important."*

- **The unlovable wound:** This is one of the most
  difficult wounds to heal. If you were constantly
  abused or mistreated as a child, you grow up
  feeling unworthy of love, which leads to
  accepting harmful environments and
  relationships. This wound is manifested in
  beliefs such as *"I am not important,"* or *"I feel like
  no one could ever truly love me for who I am,"* or *"I
  am fundamentally flawed and unlovable."* (8)

Lily was a lonely little girl with busy working parents.
She remembered coming home from school and
cooking her dinner in silence while she did her homework for the next day. As an "adult child," Lily became
accustomed to solving problems independently because
she had no one to turn to when scared or sad. Lily felt
abandoned, so when Jack came along, she felt she had
found the solution in him and wanted to hold on no
matter what.

Do you identify with any of these core emotional
wounds? How do you think these wounds play out in
your relationships today?

HOW TO RESOLVE CORE WOUNDS: TAKING PERSONAL RESPONSIBILITY FOR CHANGE

The most problematic effect of core wounds is that we tend to be attracted to people who activate them. For example, Lily had an abandonment emotional core wound, so she was attracted to someone who constantly neglected her emotions. Jack's favorite tactic was to leave the house for hours or days without even answering his phone to draw her in, which met his need of being needed but fed her wound of abandonment.

You can begin to resolve your core wounds by following this helpful advice:

- **Acknowledge your wound:** The first step in healing yourself and your relationships is to acknowledge that you have a wound(s) in the first place. When we are afraid to address our wounds, they direct our thoughts, behavior, and choices. Instead of pretending it isn't there, acknowledge and embrace the painful reality without running away from it. Take off the denial mask and be honest with yourself and the suffering you've experienced.

- **Allow yourself to feel:** Our minds are accustomed to denying or suppressing those emotions that are uncomfortable or painful until they feel numb. We think this will solve the problem, but it only does so for a short time. Emotional numbing doesn't lead to healing but to other psychological disorders, such as depression and anxiety. Healing core wounds requires acknowledging and naming your emotions and processing them without judgment.

- **Explore your attachment style:** Core emotional wounds lead to specific attachment styles in our relationships. These wounds occur when we develop harmful attachment patterns with our parents or caregivers. Lily developed an anxious attachment style; it manifested in a fear that Jack would abandon her, just as her parents had. Core wound healing can be triggered when you explore, identify, and take conscious steps to avoid these attachment styles. (7)

Lily suffered greatly from her toxic relationship with Jack. But the healing process began once she could step out of the victim position and become aware of her role in the toxicity. Lily was addicted to her relationship with Jack because she was codependent on him. She lacked self-esteem and depended on Jack to make her feel valuable and meaningful. This inability to let go of Jack was related to her core emotional wound of a fear of abandonment from childhood. Once she made room for it in her heart, Lily was ready to heal. Now it was time for closure.

MAKE IT STICK

Instructions: Take some time to reflect on the prompts and responses below to assess your role in your toxic relationship. Answer each question honestly and thoughtfully.

Did you need your partner's presence or attention to feel validated or loved daily? *Answer Yes or No. Also, elaborate on your experience in the space provided.*

How often did you fall victim to your partner's opinions? *Elaborate on your experience in the area provided.*

_____

_____

_____

_____

_____

How often do you doubt your views, ideas, and personal competence in your relationships? *Elaborate on your experience in the area provided.*

_____

_____

_____

_____

_____

Can you identify your core wounds and how they may manifest in your relationships? *Elaborate on your experience in the space provided.*

_____

_____

_____

_____

_____

What is your definition of healthy self-esteem, and how does this concept fit into the dynamics of your relationship? *Elaborate on your experience in the space provided.*

_____

_____

_____

_____

_____

How can you set healthy boundaries in your relationships? *Elaborate on your experience in the space provided.*

_____

_____

_____

_____

_____

Remember that while it's not your fault you were in a toxic relationship, understanding your role in the toxicity creates ownership and responsibility, which are essential for healing. You can find the strength to move forward from this place of humility. Writing about your experiences is also a powerful tool for clarity and healing.

3

EMBRACING THE END: CREATING CLOSURE FROM TOXIC RELATIONSHIPS

> *"Once we have achieved inner balance, we don't need closure from an outside source. We find closure in the perfection of the soul and in the balanced state of mind we have when we are fully connected with our true self."*

— CASSANDRA BLIZZARD

L eaving Jack was not the end of the relationship drama for Lily. Physically getting out of that toxic relationship and environment was a crucial step at the beginning of healing, especially because it was difficult for her to make the decision. Let's remember Lily spent a long time in shame and guilt, shutting herself off from the outside world and trying to convince herself that her misery was temporary and mostly her fault, and acted in the belief that things would soon change.

It took Lily hitting rock bottom with the toxic relationship's profoundly damaging effects left in her body and mind to see the only way out was to leave. Lily didn't take long to realize the energy and effort needed to break the attachment with Jack. Not to mention the personal healing that awaited her recovery journey.

Not surprisingly, Jack did not take the decision to leave well. His surprise, which quickly turned to deep anger, was evident from day one in his threatening text messages and constant phone calls to Lily's sister's house, where she was staying temporarily.

Jack made it very clear that he disapproved of her decision, and from that moment on, he created numerous obstacles to prevent the breakup. He refused to return Lily's belongings that she left at his house, such as clothes, letters, and toiletries. He also showed up at her work and home uninvited and even threatened to hurt himself if she didn't return.

Lily didn't understand why he was pursuing her when he didn't seem to care about her when they lived together. But even more difficult was the urge to go back to Jack. She knew going back would make her miserable. Since the beginning of the relationship, she needed to save him from his unhappiness. Lily even missed the familiar (yet toxic) routine and the sense of validation (although false) their relationship gave her, despite it being unhealthy.

Many months of bitterness, sadness, and emotional turmoil passed once Jack and Lily finally stopped speaking to each other. Over time she slowly began to feel more like her old self. She even returned to her office job, rekindled friendships from the past, and started talking openly about what had happened to her.

Eventually, after deep soul-searching and therapy, Lily realized that closure was vital for her to move on. She needed to clarify exactly why the relationship ended and everything she had been through so she could stop feeling attached to the pain and injustices she endured.

She decided to confront Jack and have one last conversation with him to put things to rest for good. However, despite her attempts to meet him in a neutral place and talk about everything, he refused to meet with her.

That's when it hit her. She needed closure to forgive herself for trusting someone who deeply hurt her. She didn't need Jack's permission, remorse, or forgiveness to be ok. She didn't need Jack to give her permission to move on. What she sought, she could find within herself.

- Why was it necessary for Lily to have closure?
- Why did Jack keep pursuing Lily?
- Why did Lily still want to be with Jack despite being miserable?
- How did Lily find closure for herself?

Getting closure is essential to more profound healing when leaving a toxic relationship, but it takes time and comes in layered insight. Closure ensures we are physically safe and psychologically and emotionally healed.

WHY LEAVING IS THE ONLY OPTION?

Even the most rational and self-reliant people can be lured into believing they can fix a troubled relationship by adjusting their behavior or finding a magical solution. Lily's story fits into the category. Deep down, she thought things would eventually work out if she tried hard enough or was more patient and understanding with Jack.

But the problem with toxic relationships is that they tend not to change. Resolution would have happened long before this tipping point if anything were to change. Toxic people create toxic cycles. Breaking out of a toxic cycle takes both partners' concerted effort, high awareness, and honesty. And these are difficult conditions to meet. (1)

Why is it so Hard to Leave?

Leaving a toxic partner is not likely to be easy. Despite a toxic relationship, a sense of codependent security is created within the dysfunction. When Lily left Jack, that codependent dysfunctional ecosystem was disrupted.

This resulted in Jack wanting to control Lily even more by constantly calling her, showing up at her work or home uninvited, and refusing to return her belongings. When a narcissistic partner is used to manipulating, lying, and controlling to get their way, these traits will escalate to get the codependent partner back in a place of dependency and control.

Breaking free from a toxic relationship is like swimming against a strong current. It may seem easier to give up and let the current take you, but the longer you stay in the water, the more exhausted and battered you become. Eventually, you realize the only way to save yourself is to fight across the current and swim toward the shore. Most importantly, get out of the water completely. This takes an enormous amount of effort and strength. Walking away from a toxic relationship is excruciating, yet always worth the energy. (2)

The Cost of Staying

Recognizing the cost of staying in a toxic relationship can be motivating. However, toxic symptoms become "normal," so seeing them as toxic and harmful is difficult. Looking at their emotionally and physically depleting nature is essential.

The first symptom Lily struggled with was **chronic fatigue.** Toxic partners are seen as energetic vampires who feed on our emotions and vitality. Lily always felt tired, unmotivated, and unable to rest or sleep well at night. She also struggled with **anxiety** and **depression** due to the emotional manipulation she suffered. However, the worst consequence she experienced was **losing her own identity.** The three years she stayed in that relationship were all about Jack and Jack alone. What he wanted, what he needed, what food Jack wanted to eat, where he wanted to go on vacation, what things she should stop saying or doing to make Jack happy. (3)

After the breakup, It took a long time for Lily to get to know herself again. Ending three years of patterns takes time. Finishing her relationship with Jack meant rebuilding her identity, including her interests, hobbies, and goals in life. The cost of leaving is great but will never exceed the cost of staying in the relationship.

THE IMPORTANCE OF CLOSURE

Creating proper closure is the ideal scenario for moving on with life after a toxic relationship. A sincere, deep, and enlightening conversation with your partner can help clarify the reasons for the breakup, process those emotions, and move toward healing.

But as mentioned earlier, toxic partners are usually reluctant to let the relationship end, much less admit the toxicity. The inability to communicate makes searching for closure much more daunting but not impossible.

The good news is that we can find closure for ourselves. And truthfully, this is the most healthy closure to find. Because it's not dependent on the feelings or actions of another. It's finding peace internally with one's self. This process helped Lily release the emotional strings and pain that kept her emotionally attached to Jack. (4)

When we give ourselves closure, we can make sense of the relationship history healthily and understand with greater clarity what led to the breakup.

Without closure, we are left vulnerable and wondering how someone we trusted could do this to us. Or worse, how can we trust ourselves not to make the same mistakes in the future?

Closure looks and feels different for everyone. But the purpose is to have a sense of understanding, completion, and peace that allows us to move through the healing process and on to the next chapters of our lives. (5)

A few months after the physical breakup, Lily couldn't stop thinking about the relationship. She was still emotionally and energetically involved, constantly checking Jack's social media and being triggered by the notifications on her phone. She felt ashamed, unloved, and inferior, remembering Jack's accusations that she was too demanding, sensitive, or dramatic.

These feelings, which made her question her self-love and worth, quickly turned into anger and resentment. Lily struggled daily with a wide range of emotions, all of which were clear signs that she needed to give herself closure. (5)

How to Give Yourself Closure

Everyone can heal from the past, no matter how long it takes. The Journal of Positive Psychology conducted an interesting study that concluded that 11 weeks after experiencing a breakup, 71% of participants began to see their past relationship positively. (6)

The first fact to be aware of is that **you don't need the other person to give you closure** to move on. If Lily had waited for Jack to heal, she would still be trapped in the painful relationship, which brings me to my next point.

The end of a relationship, especially a long or intimate one, is always difficult. There's no need to avoid the pain, grief, and sadness that will unfold. **Open your heart and mind to the grief experience** and approach it compassionately! Remember that feelings are like storms; all storms come to an end.

Once you've opened your heart to these feelings, **close the door on this person** and commit to never contacting them again, regardless of the reasons you create for doing so. Lily deleted Jack from her social media accounts and didn't respond to his attempts to contact her. While difficult, this action allowed her to focus on her future and have something else to wake up to every day. (7)

Why Your Toxic Ex May Be on Your Tail Again?

One of the things that confused Lily the most was Jack's attitude when she decided to leave him. From one day to the next, he pursued her relentlessly, even though he had mistreated her throughout their relationship.

If you're going through the same experience, don't fall into the trap of believing that your ex is sorry for what happened and will improve their behavior if you get back together.

Your ex-partner doesn't miss you. What they do miss is what you provided for them. Moreover, a study by Mogilski and Welling (2017) showed that people with narcissistic traits stayed friends with their exes out of convenience. In Jack's case, he started chasing Lily as soon as he realized he had lost control of her. These individuals hate to fail or lose because it goes against their grandiose and flawless image. (8)

Jack knew how to exploit Lily's vulnerabilities and insecurities to manipulate her into returning to him. He told her she was nothing without him and tried convincing her that she would never get a job or find a friend or boyfriend who could stand her demanding and dramatic personality. These were lies!

So always remember that if a toxic ex-partner is trying to reach you, they are most likely trying to get you back into the controlling toxic dynamic that made you want to get out of the relationship in the first place.

Why You Still Want to Be With Your Toxic Ex Despite Their Abusive Behavior?

Another common scenario after ending your toxic relationship is the urge to get back together with your ex, despite all you have suffered. Why does that happen?

Toxic relationships are like a drug addiction that is very difficult to overcome. This dynamic creates traumatic bonds resulting from shared emotional experiences, popularly known as "trauma bonding."

Our bodies become used to the emotional highs and lows we receive in our toxic relationship on a biochemical level. A study conducted by Fisher et al. revealed that people who experience intense romantic love show many of the same symptoms involved in substance addiction, including craving and emotional and physical dependence. (10)

Therefore, the only way to "detox" is to cut off any connection with them, let the pain take its course, and let it move through and out of our system. (8)

Despite the struggle, pain, and doubt that crept into her mind, Lily made the courageous decision to commit to closure. She realized she could heal from her relationship, regardless of Jack's actions, by ending contact, practicing self-compassion, making space for her feelings, and focusing on the promising future ahead.

She recognized that she couldn't continue to straddle the line between healing and relationship. This process required a wholehearted commitment. Choosing closure does not guarantee that you won't feel the hurt, sadness, and grief from the traumatic relationship that left a scar on your heart. However, committing to the journey of moving forward and healing is the only way forward. Doing the same will benefit you through the 5 Steps to Healing and Recovery From Your Toxic Relationship.

MAKE IT STICK

Instructions: Take some time to reflect on the prompts and responses below to create the closure needed from your toxic relationship. Answer each question honestly and thoughtfully.

What thoughts are coming up to convince you to get back with your ex, and how are they only a part of breaking the addiction? *Elaborate on your experience in the space provided.*

_____

_____

_____

_____

_____

What negative physical and emotional symptoms did you begin to develop through your toxic relationship? *Elaborate on your experience in the space provided.*

_____

_____

_____

_____

_____

What are you not willing to compromise when it comes down to your future relationships? *Elaborate on your experience in the space provided.*

_____

_____

_____

_____

_____

What did your partner say or do to try to get you back after the breakup? What helped you not fall for it? *Elaborate on your experience in the space provided.*

_____

_____

_____

_____

_____

What lessons can you take moving forward from your relationship experience? *Elaborate on your experience in the space provided.*

_____

_____

_____

_____

_____

I am committed to creating closure with my ended Toxic Relationship. *Explain why in the space provided.*

_____

_____

_____

_____

_____

Remember closure is a commitment to yourself. This commitment will create the foundation for giving yourself fully to the healing process. Writing about your experiences is a powerful tool for clarity and healing.

4

STEP 1: ALLOWING YOURSELF TO FEEL THE PAIN

> *"Breakups can be sad, but sometimes tears are the price we pay for a freedom we need."*

> — STEVE MARABOLI

If there is one thing you cannot avoid when you leave a toxic relationship–it's pain. No matter how hard you try to escape it, deny it, or distract yourself, the pain is there. The truth is that pain will demand your attention, so it's best not to try to ignore it.

It can come in the form of depressive symptoms, high anxiety levels, loss of appetite, or 14 hours of sleep daily. It's also common to experience compulsive mental replays of the injustices you've suffered.

After completely cutting off contact with Jack, Lily tried to adopt a matter-of-fact attitude to make up for the time she had lost. She resumed college classes and worked part-time at a department store near her sister's house.

However, the intense feelings from her experience with Jack crept back into her mind whenever she was alone, in the bathroom, driving, or cooking dinner.

Lily felt like a failure for not moving on and feeling like her old self more quickly. There was no joy to be found in her daily activities. She simply existed on autopilot. Sometimes she felt like an empty shell, and other times she felt like her heart was a raging volcano about to explode.

Jack made her feel like utter garbage, yet she felt disabled without him. This was incredibly confusing to Lily. Because of this, finding the motivation to move on seemed impossible. Even though she knew logically, she would be better off without him.

The daily struggle to avoid these painful feelings drained all of her energy. One day, exhausted and desperate, Lily decided to release control and move toward pain instead of away from it.

This may sound scary and incredibly counterintuitive. Think of it this way. Suppose you were trapped in quicksand. Naturally, you'd do your best to get out by walking, climbing, or jumping. But the more you push down on the sand, the deeper you sink. The more you struggle, push with your hands, or wiggle, the deeper you sink.

You have two choices: panic and start complaining about why you cannot get out, or lie down on the sand and make full contact with it. Instead of fighting it, create as much surface area as possible. Only then can you eventually get out of the quicksand.

It took Lily a long time to realize the only way to get over the anger, sadness, and betrayal she experienced was to...go through it.

Like Lily, you can heal from your pain by trusting the grieving process and being patient and compassionate with yourself. Finding the end to these feelings is only possible once you decide to make room for them.

- Which of these inner experiences and emotions that Lily felt were part of the emotional hangover from her breakup with Jack?
- What happened in Lily's brain during the grieving process?
- What was the healthiest way for Lily to grieve the end of her toxic relationship?

Mourning your relationship by understanding what happened in your heart after you left the toxic relationship and truly letting yourself grieve is the first of the 5 Steps to Healing and Recovering from your toxic relationship.

THE EMOTIONAL HANGOVER FROM LEAVING A TOXIC RELATIONSHIP

Have you ever woken up the day after a fun party and felt physically and emotionally drained? Well, an emotional hangover is no different from this. It happens after going through an overwhelming experience, such as a breakup. (1)

Believe it or not, the emotional hangover of leaving a toxic relationship can be harder than leaving a healthy one. The rollercoaster of emotions is intense! Deep sadness followed by intense anger at how someone who supposedly loved you treated you with such a lack of empathy can overwhelm your senses. Combined with the cluster of emotions that results from breaking a codependent bond. This emotional soup was disguised with an apathetic depression that numbed the deep pain Lily struggled with daily.

Even though these feelings are intense and painful, it's important to recognize that they are a part of the healing process. A reassuring thought helped Lily get through these overwhelming emotions. She told herself that the temporary pain of feeling her feelings was worth it if that meant she would never again have to walk on eggshells, apologize for everything she said or did, or feel guilty every day.

She committed to treating herself with compassion and patience as she worked through the emotional hang-over she was experiencing. (2)

What Happens After Narcissistic Abuse?

Before going through the healing process, it's important to recognize the effects narcissistic abuse has on your brain. A study by Bueso-Izquierdo et al. showed that the brain processes emotions differently after suffering relationship abuse. (3)

The areas of the brain associated with negative emotions showed increased activity, resulting in constantly being on edge and experiencing constant and sudden mood swings. Therefore, feeling stressed, unable to control your emotions, and overwhelmed by your feelings are all part of literally re-regulating the brain during recovery. (4)

7 Stages of Healing & Recovery After Narcissistic Abuse

The following are the seven expected stages of recovery from Narcissistic Abuse. It is important to note that this is not a linear process, which means you can move forward or backward in any of these steps, and that's okay. There's also no set amount of time expected for any part of this process. Be patient with yourself and take as much time as you need to move forward. (5)

1. **Devastation:** The first stage is realizing you've been a victim of narcissistic or toxic abuse, which can be a shocking and overwhelming experience. Lily describes it as waking up from a vivid nightmare and now seeing the lies she couldn't see before.
2. **Self-Doubt:** However, after these enlightened insights, Lily was immediately faced with self-doubt and denial of what happened. She justified Jack's actions and behavior, saying, "If she had been less dramatic or clingy...Then they may be together still and happy" This experience is also normal. It takes a while to understand the truth fully, so be patient with yourself during this time.
3. **Education:** Once Lily came to terms with reality, she educated herself about toxic

relationships and narcissistic abuse to truly understand what happened to her. Sometimes, she had more questions than answers, which is perfectly okay.

4. **Anger:** The function of anger is to remind you that your boundaries have been crossed. During this phase, Lily felt outraged at the situation she was in. Living in her sister's guest room, getting pieces of herself back, seeming like she was "behind" as she watched all her coworker friends move forward in their careers. This intense anger opened the door for other emotions to come up. While feeling angry is uncomfortable, it is a positive part of the healing process and reclaiming identity.

5. **Depression:** Lily lost interest in activities she once enjoyed. Feeling unmotivated and vulnerable is an expected part of the grieving process. Be patient as you regain emotional strength, and don't pressure yourself to be who you were before this happened. Accept this stage with compassion, knowing it's necessary to move forward. Please note it's important to seek professional help if your depression symptoms are overwhelming and you need additional support.

6. **Validation:** Recognizing and acknowledging our emotions and experiences as valid and understandable is vital for forgiveness and healing. During this stage, Lily fully understood that she was a victim of abuse and finally saw herself as a survivor. This stage felt like a huge victory after her hard work.

7. **Introspection:** The recovery process allowed Lily to embark on a deep and enlightening journey of self-discovery. She suddenly had a strong desire to understand why this abuse occurred and how she could change to prevent it from happening again in the future. At this stage, Lily better understood her emotional needs and boundaries and began to treat herself with love and respect.

HOW TO MOURN A BREAKUP SO YOU CAN TRULY HEAL

The main reason time is needed to mourn after a breakup is to reflect on the experience you've been through, recharge your energy and detoxify your nervous system from the intense and traumatic emotions you lived through for so long. Taking time without dating or doing anything that can hinder the healing process is important. The point is to become re-acquainted with yourself. Becoming comfortable in your own skin again ensures you move into life and future relationships from a place of stability instead of brokenness, neediness, and lack.

This mourning period allowed Lily to deal with the emotional baggage of her relationship with Jack, which was heavy. The pain that comes feels the same as mourning the death of a loved one. All the hopes, dreams, and experiences associated with the relationship died when Lily finally cut Jack out of her life.

All the space created in her mind and heart that made her feel so anxious soon became an opportunity to figure out her interests and desires. Lily was ready to rebuild her identity by letting the grieving process move through her life. (6)

How to Grieve in a Healthy Way

Hopefully, by now, you can see the wisdom in not running from your feelings but just letting yourself feel and grieve. Despite the unhealthy nature of a toxic relationship, the break is still a loss, and it hurts. The following are healthy strategies for coping with a breakup that will help you accept and move through the grieving process without becoming overwhelming or unnecessarily prolonged. (7)

- **Don't fight your feelings:** This is the first and most important piece of advice. A wide range of uncomfortable, painful, and difficult feelings will arise after a breakup as a natural response to the experience. Expect to feel sad, anxious, angry, resentful, and regretful, just to name a few. That's okay. All emotions are valid, and the more you let them in, the less overwhelming their long-term effects will be.

- **Express your feelings openly:** Talking or writing about your feelings surrounding the breakup is a powerful way to deal with them. Sharing experiences with supportive people we love can play a large role in our sense of relief and understanding. When Lily finally shared her relationship struggles with her sister and friends, she realized she wasn't alone and needed healing support.

- **Prioritize self-care:** This step was one of the hardest for Lily. She realized that Jack rarely asked her what she wanted or needed throughout their relationship. As a result, she became accustomed to neglecting her own emotional needs. After she cut him out of her life, it took her a while to determine her needs. Eventually, she committed to eating well, getting enough sleep, and meeting all her basic needs. Prioritizing self-care is the best tool to move quickly through recovery.

- **Get back into a routine:** Going through this breakup turned Lily's life upside down. Finding and sticking to a routine was essential for her to feel more emotionally stable as she grieved. Similarly, returning to a routine can help you avoid feeling overwhelmed by your sense of chaos and feeling out of control.

- **Indulge yourself:** Doing activities that brought Lily joy was low on her list of priorities. But finding ways to smile and laugh was necessary. During your grieving process, go to your favorite restaurant, watch your favorite movie, spend time with your friends, or take a short trip to a city you love... Indulge in all the activities that bring joy and nourishment to your life.

- **Don't pressure yourself:** Expecting to be perfectly functional during this challenging period is not only too idealistic, but it can lead to feelings of failure and disappointment. Lily wanted to resume her studies and graduate as quickly as possible. But when she was dragged down by anxiety and depression, this goal made her feel even more pressured and inadequate. Give yourself some slack and accept that your best right now may not be your best when you aren't grieving. Take your time.

- **Don't lose faith in people:** Just because you had a toxic partner doesn't mean everyone is the same. Don't let your toxic relationship keep you from meeting trustworthy, honest, loving, and worthwhile people. Take as much time as you need to be alone, but don't deny yourself the opportunity to meet someone special in the future.

- **Don't seek revenge:** The idea of revenge can be very tempting at some point in your grief journey. When Lily could acknowledge her abuse, she wanted to unblock Jack's number and tell him all the terrible things going through her mind. But doing so would have the consequence of letting him back into her circle by getting in touch with him, which was one of the things she agreed not to do. Don't get caught up in the heat of the moment. Trust that this feeling of revenge will pass. Don't just stuff the feelings, either. You may try writing a letter with everything you would like to say, then burning it as a symbol that all the drama is over and done.

- **Examine what you can learn from this experience:** Exploring what you've learned from the relationship can be a positive way to accept the grieving process. However, avoid the temptation to beat yourself up or blame yourself for how things turned out. Instead, ask yourself how this experience is helping you to become a better, stronger, or more authentic version of yourself. (7).

It's okay not to feel okay during the first step of recovery and healing from your toxic relationship. Fighting the intense and painful feelings that arise during this stage will only prolong the suffering and make it seem more overwhelming.

Imagine playing a game of cards and being dealt a specific hand. It might not be the hand you were hoping for (the breakup), but your chances of winning depend on how well you play the cards you have rather than the ones you wish you had been dealt. In other words, focusing on making the most of what you have, rather than dwelling on what you don't have, will give you the best chance of success.

It's also important to remember that grief does not have a defined timeline. The grieving process is unique to everyone, so don't pressure yourself to be the same person you were before the breakup. This experience has changed you, as it should! Allow all these powerful and intense emotions to flow through your heart and help you see life from a wiser and more resilient perspective. Then, you'll be ready to cultivate self-love and finally forgive yourself.

MAKE IT STICK

Instructions: Please rate how you feel after reading each question by choosing one of the following options. Answer each question honestly and thoughtfully.

1. How much are you having trouble accepting the loss of your relationship?

Not at all............0   Somewhat............1   A lot............2

2. How much does your grief still interfere with your everyday routine?

Not at all............0   Somewhat............1   A lot............2

3. How much are you having thoughts of your ex-partner that bother you?

Not at all............0   Somewhat............1   A lot............2

4. Are there things you used to do with your ex that you avoid? For example, going to certain restaurants, venues, or hobbies you used to do together.

Not at all............0   Somewhat............1   A lot............2

5. How much have you felt cut off or distant from other people since your breakup?

Not at all............0   Somewhat............1   A lot............2

A score of 4 or more suggests that you may be experiencing complicated grief. (M.K. Shear, personal communication, January 2014). You may benefit from a mental health assessment to determine if you need professional help during your recovery.

6. Which of the 7 Steps of Healing & Recovery are you in? Which one do you think has been the hardest so far? *Write about your experience below.*

_____

_____

_____

_____

_____

7. What does it mean to you to allow yourself to feel? *Write about how you can be compassionate to yourself during this process of feeling.*

_____

_____

_____

_____

_____

8. How well do you take care of yourself during the grieving process? What activities do you consider to be self-care?

_____

_____

_____

_____

_____

Remember that grieving the end of a relationship is a natural and emotionally intense process that doesn't have a specific time frame. Allow yourself to feel all the feelings and be as compassionate as possible.

5

STEP 2: STRENGTHENING THE INNER SELF THROUGH FORGIVENESS AND SELF-LOVE

> *"As I began to love myself, I found that anguish and emotional suffering were only warning signs that I was living against my own truth."*

— CHARLIE CHAPLIN

Once Lily opened the doors to her wide and deep range of emotions and let them into her heart, she realized how little attention she paid to her inner world not just during her relationship with Jack, but throughout her life.

Lily's feelings were never validated or encouraged in her childhood. As a result, she became accustomed to asking for and receiving affection by pleasing other people. Subconsciously, she was trying to earn their love by helping them first.

Jack was Lily's first "real" boyfriend. Her learned pattern of serving others to deserve love created a recipe for disaster in an intimate relationship. This first exposure to intimacy, combined with her over-serving inclinations, naturally created emotional codependency and low self-esteem. Lily gave Jack all her energy, emotion, and time to the point of losing herself in the relationship. She was dumping all her love into a pit, expecting to receive love back, but it didn't work that way with Jack. Leaving her drained, empty, and desperate for love.

A core belief that dominated Lily's thoughts, feelings, and decisions was "I am not enough." Unfortunately, this lens through which she viewed reality led to her over-serving during her relationship with Jack and created a lonely and miserable feeling of inadequacy during the first few months after her breakup.

Although she wanted to feel okay about being single, deep down, she felt a large part of her was empty and lost. As painful as this experience was, with time and a shift in perspective, she realized this emptiness turned out to be a blank slate. Yes, Lily felt lost and confused, but she also had the opportunity to discover who she was for the first time in her life.

Through self-care and self-love, Lily learned to recognize and meet her emotional needs in a way that Jack, her parents, and she had never done in the past. In addition, through self-love, Lily learned to heal from all the toxic relationships in her life.

This was the beginning of a long and rewarding journey of finding and setting boundaries, communicating her needs assertively, and letting go of the power she allowed others to hold over her.

Most importantly, Lily learned to forgive herself. She embraced her inner child and looked back with compassion instead of shame or guilt for falling in love with Jack. She saw how she placed all her innocent hopes of a happily ever after and trust in Jack, and she forgave herself for not knowing better.

For the first time, the belief that "I am not enough" began to shift and be reprogrammed to "I am enough" through Lily's decision to love herself.

- What actions and decisions changed in Lily's life after she began practicing self-love?
- How did self-forgiveness help Lily heal?
- How did Lily overcome the emotional flashbacks left by the relationship?
- What changed in Lily's life when she started loving herself?

Shifting doubt and self-loathing to self-love, self-compassion, and self-forgiveness is vital in healing from a toxic relationship.

WHY YOU MUST FORGIVE YOURSELF TO HEAL FROM NARCISSISTIC ABUSE

After coming to terms with the fact that Lily was in an abusive relationship, anger and shame set in, creating questions in her mind like, "Why did I have to endure so much pain? Why didn't I see it before?" In short, a constant barrage of judgment against herself and Jack became part of her daily life in an almost obsessive way.

Forgiving herself was not easy. She could say it with her mind, but her heart took a few more steps to get there. Her heart held on to resentment as a justification for how poorly she was treated. Psychologically, the prolonged harbored anger helped her feel in control. But the truth is, holding onto anger is like drinking poison but expecting the other person to die. She knew the cankerous feelings were only hurting her.

However, pressuring a state of forgiveness wasn't the solution either. That's when Lily heard about the concept of self-forgiveness, which seemed simple in theory but challenging to implement.

Self-forgiveness is consciously letting go of guilt, shame, or resentment toward ourselves for past mistakes, wrongdoings, or failures. Some people believe they must accept blame to learn the lessons of their experiences, but that belief only heaps shame on the "wrong-doer."

Here's what's flawed about that notion. No one intentionally hurts themselves or others on purpose (at least most of humanity). So, how can you take the blame for something where you were innocent? Knowledgeable intent is required for responsibility to rest on someone. You didn't know any better. And if you did know better, then you wouldn't have done it.

Self-forgiveness is about taking responsibility for our actions, acknowledging the harm we have caused, and ultimately offering ourselves compassion and understanding that we didn't know any better. And this usually happens AFTER the actions are over. Shaming ourselves for something in the past that is unchangeable is counterproductive. So forgiveness is necessary.

Self-forgiveness can be a powerful tool for healing the emotional wounds left by a toxic relationship and moving forward in a positive direction. It is a process that requires self-reflection, empathy, and a willingness to let go of negative self-judgments.

It may feel strange or uncomfortable at first because your mind is so used to being in a constant fight or flight state resulting from the toxic relationship. This fight or flight state of stress creates the feeling that everything you've done is "wrong," which again creates a shame cycle that's not helpful. However, learning to accept soft and gentle feelings and understanding is needed to heal. Compassion and self-forgiveness are the way to welcome those tender feelings into your daily existence and create the actual change required to move on.

Therefore, practicing self-forgiveness as often and as consistently as possible is essential. Just like Lily, your mind will try to take you back to those places where judgment and hatred creep into your heart. When this happens, consciously let it go without getting caught up in the anger. Be as gentle and kind to yourself as possible during this process, knowing that you will feel better with time and compassionate reinforcement.

Instead of trying to find reasons or excuses to shame the seemingly negative emotions, we choose to embrace our "bad self" with kindness and understanding, allowing it to be a part of who we are. Remember, those feelings of anger are there to protect you from getting hurt again.

Shaming your protector is not helpful. Thank the protector, but encourage the protector to let down their guard. This frees us from the pain of self-judgment or avoidance and acknowledges our human imperfections. It is essential to recognize that we did the best we could at the time and that no one intentionally seeks to be unhappy. (1)

How to Forgive Yourself

When Lily ended her toxic relationship, she quickly realized how empty her life had become. She had no passion for her career, lost all her friends, and had no self-confidence. This made it easy to beat herself up about what happened, claiming she lost time.

These thoughts were like a giant billboard constantly flashing in Lily's mind. "How could I have been so stupid?" or "How could I let this happen?" or "I have completely ruined my life." And just as was mentioned above, these feelings are real but only create shame. So recognize first that they are valid and forgive yourself for your position. But, again, you didn't know any better.

Forgiving yourself is a tough step and is more like one thousand little steps. You may need to forgive yourself multiple times a day. That's okay! There's no wrong way to forgive yourself; you just need to do it repeatedly until you see clearly that you wouldn't be where you are if you knew better. So you deserve compassion, mercy, grace, and the opportunity to move forward.

Repeatedly forgiving yourself is truly important to go through the healing and recovery process in a healthy way. This exercise below is something I've found helpful in this process:

First, **write down exactly how you feel you have let yourself down.** This is your moment to get it all off your chest and pour it out without anything holding you back.

Next, **write down how you feel about what you wrote above.** Again, you must connect with the hatred, pain, or anger at this time, as acknowledging these emotions is necessary to transform them.

Then, **write down the following:** "Despite the pain I have caused myself, I recognize that deep down, I have given myself an invaluable opportunity to understand and heal my unresolved issues. This, in turn, will allow me to build an authentic, fulfilling, and joyful life."

Now write down all the **new positive belief systems** about this challenging experience that you can now commit to creating.

The final step is to feel **gratitude**. Write out: "I express deep gratitude towards myself for collaborating in creating these experiences that have led me to find my way back home to myself and achieve complete healing."

This helps you feel the essence of the statement. Remember, gratitude is a powerful tool in promoting healing. (2)

OVERCOMING EMOTIONAL FLASHBACKS

Emotional flashbacks can quickly pull us back into intense feelings that lead us into a shame cycle before we know what's happening. These powerful feelings associated with our toxic relationship can hinder cultivating self-love and forgiveness.

Emotional flashbacks are intense and overwhelming feelings that occur in response to specific triggers or events that may resemble past traumatic experiences or emotional states. For example, emotional flashbacks can be triggered by various stimuli, such as a particular smell, sound, image, or situation that unconsciously reminds you of a past emotional wound.

These feelings accompanied Lily on her journey of recovery and healing from her toxic relationship.

Rather than deny or hide from them, she learned to work through them by following these steps.

- **Acknowledge to yourself: "I am experiencing a flashback."** Memories, thoughts, and emotions cannot harm you, even though they often feel as accurate as the actual event. Whenever one of these flashbacks returns, allow them to appear without controlling them, knowing they will take a few moments to disappear. While you wait, focus on your breathing. Follow your in-breath as your abdomen rises and your out-breath as your abdomen falls.
- **Remind yourself: "I may feel scared, but I am not currently in danger."** I am on the other side of the experience. What happened is past, and I am no longer in danger. This practice helps the brain put your traumatic experience back in its proper place in the past instead of the trauma insisting on living in the present.
- **Recognize and honor your boundaries:** Never allow anyone to abuse you again. However, you can set clear boundaries and not allow anyone to cross them. We will focus more on this in a couple of chapters.

- **Comfort your inner child by speaking to them reassuringly:** My inner child has always felt misunderstood by those around them. Assure your inner child that you acknowledge their feelings and that they will never feel alone again. It's your responsibility to parent and nurture your most tender feelings. Don't give or expect that power to be given to someone outside you.

- **Build safe relationships and seek support from trusted individuals:** Your family and friends who have not had a similar experience can sometimes be disempowering. Building a solid support network of people who have been through similar abusive relationships is vital to healing. You can also educate your loved ones who you feel safe sharing with about flashbacks so that they can help you through this difficult time.

- **Identify the specific triggers that lead to your flashbacks:** Flashbacks don't just come out of nowhere, although sometimes they feel that way. Identify the contexts, people, or thoughts that trigger this response in your body to eliminate them from your daily life or prepare for them when they come.

- **Be patient with yourself throughout the healing process:** Flashbacks are like waves. Emotions begin, peak in intensity, and subside until they are gone. Allow this process to happen, even if it seems frightening. The more space you give it, the faster it will end.
- **Do not blame or criticize yourself for experiencing a flashback:** Flashbacks happen even when you don't want them to. Hating or shaming yourself for them only hinders the healing process. Practice self-compassion, and remember you do not control these waves of emotion. And that it's not necessary or prudent to control everything to heal. (3)

SELF-LOVE CAN HELP YOU

As Lily continued to take small steps toward recovery and healing, she soon realized that self-love was the key to regaining the identity she longed to feel and proclaim.

Loving herself was just as powerful an antidote, if not better, than any medicine, therapy, or advice anyone gave her. Self-love made her realize she was worth more than the judgments and demands and much better off without the breadcrumbs of affection that Jack had offered her over the past few years.

Self-love allowed Lily to express her desires first to herself and then to others, which was one of the greatest triumphs and breakthroughs of her healing process. All that introspection, self-doubt, hatred, resentment, and depression allowed her to lay the foundation for a new version of herself. It was like a tree of insight revealing the truth as it fell inside her. The tree of her old self could never be put back up again. Because of this newfound awareness and desire to treat herself and be treated by others differently, she would never let anyone destroy her again. (4)

HEALING FROM NARCISSISTIC ABUSE THROUGH SELF-LOVE

At first, the concept of self-love was foreign to Lily, and she struggled to understand what it meant to prioritize her wants and needs. In addition, the idea of having feelings and desires seemed daunting, and she needed help navigating them.

It took time and effort to truly understand the importance of self-love and how it could catalyze her recovery. She had to rewire her thought process and pay close attention to herself to ensure it was safe for her to experience and express emotions. Nevertheless, it was a revolutionary and crucial attitude that allowed Lily to begin healing and finding joy again.

- **Embrace self-love and idealize yourself:**
  Despite the toxic aspects of her relationship
  with Jack, Lily could not deny that there were
  moments of bliss in the beginning. Jack made
  her feel cherished and adored like no one else
  before him. Showering her with thoughtful
  gifts and flooding her with compliments that
  left her feeling like the most important person
  in the world, while sharing thrilling
  experiences in and out of the bedroom. She was
  under his spell. As Lily embarked on her self-
  care journey, she consciously tried to remember
  and make those special moments her own. She
  sifted through the memories of her unique
  dates, the heartfelt words he used, and the
  tender gestures he made, and she reclaimed
  them as part of her own story by similarly
  treating herself with joyous experiences. In
  short, treat yourself as the most important
  person in the universe until your brain believes
  it too! Don't wait for someone else to validate
  your greatness.
- **Triangulate your story:** Overcoming doubt is
  one of the most difficult challenges for abuse
  survivors. In Lily's case, she constantly
  questioned whether her experiences were real
  or if she was overreacting. It wasn't easy, but

talking to others who had been through similar situations helped her overcome her self-doubt. By triangulating her story with theirs, she found the strength and courage to move forward in the recovery process.

- **Find balance in life's swings:** Expect ups and downs in your journey of recovery and healing. Taking care of yourself also means allowing different emotions to arise, whether pleasant or unpleasant. For example, there were times when she spent whole days in bed and other times when she felt safe and excited to go out with friends. Both are okay.

- **Express your emotions:** Since Lily never expressed her feelings in the past, finding creative ways to do so became crucial to her recovery—Journaling, painting, and even screaming emotions while hiking became essential tools in her healing process. By acknowledging and openly expressing her feelings, Lily experienced profound relief and release.

- **Enhance your intuition:** Intuition is our inner compass that's always there but appears only when we pay enough attention to our feelings and desires. When Lily was with Jack, she never asked herself what she wanted. She had no standards of what was right or wrong. She simply focused on following his lead and making him happy, and that was her barometer of what was right. She went too long without realizing she was in a terrible situation. Listening to this "sixth" sense helped her make decisions based on her core values and happiness instead of other people's expectations.

- **Let go and surrender to the Universe:** You don't have to be religious to believe that a higher power is supporting you. In Lily's case, trusting the universe and surrendering to the feeling that everything she was going through was for her greater good gave her the strength to keep going. The more she trusted that power, the more doors opened in her path, showing her–she was not alone.

- **Develop a clear self-image:** The feeling of not being important didn't start with her relationship with Jack. As mentioned, Lily's feelings were never validated growing up, so her self-image was weak and vague. Learning to see and compliment herself on her positive qualities and accepting the compliments she received from others was an uncomfortable but necessary step in rebuilding her self-esteem.

- **Practice mindful self-compassion:** Mindfulness is simply about being present, and fully accepting emotions and thoughts, even uncomfortable ones. Taking time to stop and observe what was going on from the inside out was the easiest way to uncover the thought patterns leading to self-destructive behaviors. But before she could feel bad about her mistakes, she had to accept them, which fully opened the doors of self-compassion.
- **Embrace self-care as a way of life:** Lily always considered herself empathetic and compassionate to the people and animals around her. But when she became aware of her inner dialogue, she realized there was a very aggressive side to her. That's when she consciously decided to treat herself the same way she treats the people she loves most, practicing not allowing any words of hate or discouragement to judge her struggles. (5)

Forgiving herself was not easy, but it was the only way Lily could connect with self-love meaningfully. In the end, no matter how much advice she read or followed, seeing herself through more compassionate eyes was a crucial step in her recovery and healing. She had to put it into practice. Moreover, it allowed her to begin the long journey of overcoming the emotional flashbacks from her toxic relationship with Jack.

As Lily began to love herself, she realized the importance of asking for help. A safe place to express herself and get professional advice became essential in recovery.

MAKE IT STICK

Instructions: Take some time to reflect on the following prompts to work on your self-forgiveness and self-love. Answer each question honestly and thoughtfully.

Take a moment to reflect and write about where you unintentionally shame yourself, even though you were innocent and "didn't know any better." *Whatever you write, this is the area where you need to practice self-forgiveness.*

_____

_____

_____

_____

_____

What actions can you take today to practice self-love? *Expound in the space provided below.*

_____

_____

_____

_____

_____

What new positive belief systems can you commit to creating today? *Expound in the space provided below.*

_____

_____

_____

_____

_____

Give yourself three honest and sincere compliments in the space provided.

_____

_____

_____

_____

_____

How much do you listen to your inner voice when making decisions? Describe an experience where following your intuition led you in the right direction.

_____

_____

_____

_____

_____

What do you need to do daily for your well-being (physical, emotional, and mental)? *Expound in the space provided below.*

Remember that the relationship you have with yourself is as important or more important than any other relationship in your life. So nurture it with kindness, patience, and compassion to lay the foundation for a solid and lasting bond with yourself.

6

STEP 3 - SEEKING SUPPORT FROM PROFESSIONALS IN HEALING

> *"Do not suffer in silence. Somebody somewhere is willing and prepared to help in any way to encourage, empower, and support you."*
>
> — GERMANY KENT

Lily was taught to be strong and to "shake off" her bad feelings. Asking for help was seen as a sign of weakness or even needless whining. She would think, "Other people probably had more problems to deal with than she did." Her parents were experts at denial, never talking about how "bad" they felt, although the tension could be cut with a knife during awkward silent dinners when neither looked up from their respective plates.

As the months passed after her breakup, Lily realized going about the healing and recovery journey alone was difficult. She needed additional support and guidance to overcome the trauma she experienced, and admitting this to herself was as tricky as it was relieving. That's when she decided to call a therapist recommended by a former coworker.

Lily called the therapist. Her hands were sweating, as always, before exposing herself to a situation outside her comfort zone. Every time the phone rang, her heart skipped a beat, and she had to repeat everything in her head a few times before summoning the courage to ask for help. However, the anxiety subsided when she heard the kind and understanding voice on the other end of the phone.

Her sister's and friends' support was one thing, but hearing the words and feedback of a kind and unbiased mental health professional was another. Lily's feelings and experiences were explained, understood, and validated for the first time.

Instead of feeling like she was burdening others with her problems, Lily understood that her therapy sessions were as important as eating well or going to the gym.

Together with her therapist, they worked on unpacking Lily's emotions and processing the trauma she experienced. Over time, Lily began to feel more empowered and in control of her life. Most importantly, she felt more comfortable in her own skin.

Lily realized that seeking psychological help wasn't a sign of weakness but rather a sign of strength. It took courage to admit she needed it, and she was proud of herself for taking that step.

- What initially made it so hard for her to ask for help?
- How did she overcome her fear of asking for help?
- What signs made Lily know she had found the right therapist?

Seeking psychological help requires the release of the prejudices that your family and society have installed about therapy in your mind. Once this happens, you will be ready to find the right therapist to help you become the best version of yourself.

WHAT ARE THE BENEFITS OF SEEKING HELP?

Mental health has been stigmatized and shrouded for many generations. However, this does not make mental illness disappear; quite the contrary. According to the National Alliance on Mental Health, 21% of U.S. adults experienced mental illness in 2020, so it is important to normalize seeking help and support for our mental well-being.

There is no question that depression, anxiety, trauma, and other psychological and emotional issues must be addressed professionally. But taking that first step to enlist help is not easy for anyone.

Many times Lily doubted whether she needed to seek help or not. After all, she still needed to be informed about the benefits and importance of seeking help at the right time. Seeking professional help is not a sign of alarm or weakness. On the contrary, it indicates you are ready to take control of your life.

First, dealing with a breakup, especially a toxic one, is a devastating and isolating experience. The grieving process alone isolated Lily from social contact while she recovered. Having the **guidance and advice** of a therapist and a community that understands what you are going through can be a real game changer. It normalized the pain experienced through the breakup and grief process; instead of second-guessing or shaming thoughts and actions.

Getting help may also **reduce the risk for other medical problems,** such as sleep or hormonal disorders because symptoms are managed more effectively.

In addition, your therapist is trained to help you **develop appropriate coping strategies** to navigate challenging experiences with greater self-awareness and confidence.

Plus, through psychological help, you can **gain a deeper understanding of your thoughts, feelings, and behaviors.** This can help you identify problematic patterns, make positive changes in different areas of your life, and ensure unwanted patterns aren't repeated. (1)

Why Asking For Help Is Okay

A survey conducted by Study Finds revealed that 73% of people in the United States don't ask for help when starting something new. This speaks to a society used to being driven by the mandate to solve problems individually and not "bother" the people around them. As a result, most Western societies do not turn to their support system to move forward, even when they are struggling and lack support.

We tend to take the Western approach regarding our emotional well-being, forgetting that **mental and emotional health struggles are a natural part of being human.** We are all expected to experience difficulties in life. They are meant to help us grow. Pretending to have a conflict-free life is as fanciful as trying to cover the sun with a finger. This pretending also creates unnecessary suffering from self-judgment, wondering why life is so difficult when everyone else seems fine. The reality is we all struggle. We all need help.

Another reason it's okay to ask for help is because of the **unreliable nature of our thought patterns.** We interpret life through specific lenses that are not objective, and those thoughts can cause us to get stuck in negative patterns. Worst of all, we believe these thoughts just because we think them rather than treating them as hypotheses to be tested against reality.

When we are too overwhelmed by our negative thinking and emotional states, we can feel that things will never improve. It's critical to remember that **all thoughts, emotions, and actions are temporary.** Seeking professional help can help put things into perspective and navigate inner states more effectively.

In short, **asking for help is a sign of strength and wisdom.** It shows you want to regain control of reactions and decisions instead of letting negative experiences restrain your life. (2)

Possible Reasons Why Asking for Help is Hard When Distressed

One main reason why some people find it so difficult to ask for help goes back to our childhood. Our upbringing and caregivers' approach to life significantly impacts our thoughts, beliefs, and attitudes. In Lily's case, the phrase "stop whining, pick yourself up, and move on" was why she never took a compassionate approach to her distress.

Many of us have experienced similar messages from our parents or peers. These mindsets likely stem from a legacy stemming back from previous generations where survival and hard work precede emotional well-being. Therefore, Lily's first therapy work was to re-establish the importance of her mental health and what that meant.

But beyond upbringing and family background, the social and personal mandates we place on our shoulders also lead to overlooking mental health. Many fear losing their careers or being ostracized from their social circles for disclosing their mental health struggles. They fear being seen as unfit, weak, or strange and prefer to bear the emotional, physical, and spiritual burden of dealing with personal challenges alone.

When Lily challenged these beliefs with reality, she found that the response from her social circles was very different from what she expected. Her friends and colleagues were compassionate and open to her experience, which made her healing journey much easier and more collaborative. (3)

Refusing to ask for help may seem like a quick fix to avoid embarrassment or judgment, but it can lead to more significant problems in the long run. Keeping quiet and not expressing your emotional needs can worsen your symptoms and isolate you from those around you. Lily challenged negative assumptions about herself by asking for help, making it part of her daily interactions. Asking for help at the office allowed her to delegate some of her responsibilities and strengthen her work alliances. Similarly, at home, Lily became accustomed to telling her sister about her day and asking for advice, turning their relationship into a haven where she could find support and be her true self. This significantly improved her self-esteem and confidence in dealing with daily challenges.

This decision helped her understand how others respond to her requests. It also led her to meet new people and strengthen the bonds with those she knew. In short, asking for help increased Lily's confidence and ability to handle uncomfortable situations.

FINDING A MENTAL HEALTH PROFESSIONAL YOU CAN TRUST

Beyond your therapist's experience and expertise, which are extremely important, your connection with them is key to achieving positive therapeutic outcomes, including improved mental health and overall well-being.

An essential aspect of psychotherapy is the **therapeutic alliance**, which refers to the collaborative and trusting relationship between a therapist and a client. This connection helps create a safe and supportive environment where you can openly explore and address your mental health concerns.

Lily would have struggled to open her heart and share her deepest secrets and intimacies without her therapist's sensitive, caring, and straightforward voice. She was not used to talking about her feelings and intimate experiences with other people, not even her close friends.

Her therapist, Dr. Garcia, had a unique way of making her feel seen and heard. She listened to her stories with deep attention, something Lily had never experienced before. Dr. Garcia also had a kind and gentle way of responding to all of Lily's doubts and concerns, so the fear of appearing doubtful quickly faded away. She never judged Lily but helped her explore her thoughts and feelings, even the most complex ones, with curiosity, understanding, and compassion.

At the same time, her **expertise and treatment orientation** made Lily feel safe enough to trust and commit to the professional therapy journey. Lily made sure that Dr. Garcia had experience with cases similar to hers, such as relationship toxicity and trauma. This ensured that the therapist knew what she was doing and could give her the best advice and guidance for healing.

If you're also looking for a therapist, don't hesitate to **check their credentials** and **ask for their therapeutic orientation.** Many psychologists combine different approaches, but knowing the theoretical basis will help you better understand the length of treatment and interventions needed.

For example, Psychoanalysis typically involves long-term treatment, often spanning several years. In contrast, Cognitive Behavioral Therapy (CBT) is typically a shorter-term intervention that can be completed in a few months. This difference is because psychoanalysis is a more in-depth and exploratory therapy approach to address unconscious conflicts. In contrast, CBT focuses more on identifying and changing specific thoughts and behaviors contributing to our problem and is often used to address more immediate concerns.

However, all therapeutic orientations are equally effective, depending on your preferences and needs.

But one of the essential pieces of advice when choosing a therapy and therapist is to **trust your gut.** No matter how many credentials or areas of expertise your therapist has, feel free to make another choice if the connection or therapeutic alliance doesn't feel right. You are essentially interviewing potential options. Don't feel pressure to just say yes to the first person you talk to unless it feels right. This is your therapy journey, so honor it with the right match. (4)

Consider these inquiries when selecting a therapist: (4)

- Does the therapist show genuine concern for you and your issues?
- Do you sense the therapist understands your perspective?
- Does the therapist acknowledge and accept you for who you are?
- Are you comfortable with sharing personal information with this therapist?
- Can you be candid and open with the therapist without pretending to be someone else?
- Is the therapist attentive when you speak, without interrupting, judging, or criticizing you?

- Does the therapist understand your emotions and underlying message?
- Do you feel heard by the therapist?
- Does the therapist explain the possible modalities for treatment and the pros and cons of why a certain one may be the best for your situation?

What to Avoid When Seeking Therapy

Finding the right match may not be easy initially, especially if you come from a toxic relationship with unmet needs. Be aware of the following red flags that may indicate your psychologist is not right for you.

- **Your therapist specializes in everything:** Therapists who claim to be experts in every therapy area are not ideal. When you seek therapy, you have specific needs requiring a specialized therapist. A specialty will ensure they can provide the most effective treatment to meet your needs.
- **Your therapist claims they can "cure" you:** There's no quick fix for mental health issues, and therapy isn't a cure. Progress in therapy can be slow and nonlinear, and it usually involves managing the symptoms of your

mental health condition rather than finding a "cure." So if a therapist claims they can cure you, they're probably making unrealistic promises, and it's best to find a different option.

- **Your therapist has inappropriate boundaries:** A therapist should always maintain professional boundaries with clients. Yes, therapy can feel comforting, but this doesn't mean a therapist can cross the line and try to become your friend. It's also inappropriate for therapists to arrange informal meetings outside the office.
- **You don't feel good in their presence:** Feeling comfortable and respected is essential in a therapeutic relationship. While a good therapist may challenge you to confront difficult emotions, you should never feel judged or unsupported. If you feel uneasy or uncomfortable around your therapist, finding a new one is probably best. (5)

Overall, therapy was a vital hinge that catapulted Lily's recovery journey. She gained insight into her unconscious motivations, patterns of behavior, and beliefs about herself and the world around her. With her therapist's help, she could confront and work through the complex emotions and experiences left by her toxic relationship and develop new coping strategies and ways of thinking that better served her well-being.

Before entering therapy, Lily had only begun building a small part of her identity. If she were a drawing on a blank canvas, she would have entered therapy as vague, faint, soft brush strokes outlining a slightly ghostly figure of herself.

After therapy, Lily transformed from a sketch on a blank canvas to a richly-colored painting filled with vivid shapes and inspiring values. She felt a renewed sense of purpose and motivation to continue growing and expanding her sense of self. She was ready to leave that painting and build herself out of more substantial, enduring materials like marble, stone, or diamonds. In other words, she gained a solid foundation and a deeper understanding of herself and was ready to reclaim her lost identity for good.

MAKE IT STICK

Instructions: Read and answer the following questions truthfully. This questionnaire is designed to help you reflect and assess whether or not you need professional help at this time in your life.

1. Are you having trouble concentrating?

    Yes   No

2. Are your friends and family expressing concern about you?

    Yes   No

3. Are you experiencing difficulty sleeping?

    Yes   No

4. Does nothing seem to excite you?

    Yes   No

5. Are you feeling isolated and alone?

    Yes   No

6. Are you frequently getting sick?

    Yes   No

7. Are you turning to substance abuse to cope?

Yes   No

8. Have you experienced a traumatic event?

Yes   No

If you answered yes to more than 4 of the following questions, it is time to consider seeking treatment.

If the questionnaire leads you to **seek out professional help**, write down a specific time when you will make space to find the right therapist for you.

_____

_____

_____

_____

_____

If the questionnaire leads you **not to need help at this time**, then write down the list of close people in your life whom you can trust, communicate with, and ask for support along your journey.

_____

_____

_____

_____

_____

Remember, asking for help is not a sign of weakness or defeat. On the contrary, this courageous step means you are ready to take responsibility for your actions and move forward to a fulfilling life. Furthermore, asking for help demonstrates your commitment to your inner journey and your love and respect for your mental health and well-being.

"There is power in telling your story. There is power in sharing your pain. There is power in letting someone else know they're not alone in their struggle."

— J.S. PARK

At the beginning of the book, we talked about how toxic relationships are so prevalent in our society, which made me realize that sharing these strategies would help others heal and overcome the toxicity they are experiencing in their life–and it was the driving force behind writing this book.

We can learn from the mistakes of our past, as well as the mistakes of others. But we can also learn by sharing our experiences...and this is where you, as a reader, have a chance to be part of the teaching process for those who may also be trying to heal from a toxic relationship.

Many survivors of toxic relationships have turned their experiences into opportunities to help others heal and overcome. So, likewise, you have the chance to help others find their way to healing with this book.

By leaving a review of this book on Amazon, you'll show others struggling after leaving a toxic relationship where they can find the guidance they're looking for. Simply by telling other readers how this book helped you and what they can expect to find inside, you'll set them on the road to healing and overcoming their own toxic relationships.

Thank you for your support. There may be much more work on your healing journey, but this is an excellent start to the bright and free future you're headed for. Sharing what we know is the best way to empower others to regain control of their lives. (11)

Scan the QR code below for a quick review!

7

STEP 4: RECLAIMING YOUR IDENTITY IN THE AFTERMATH OF A TOXIC RELATIONSHIP

> *"The only true happiness lies in knowing who you are ... and making peace with it."*
>
> — LAURELL K. HAMILTON

After the breakup, Lily had a hard time enjoying things she once loved because they reminded her of Jack. So to distract herself from the pain, she filled her days with all kinds of chores and activities that kept her busy to avoid thinking about him.

Lily soon ran out of tasks to do. It was a Saturday afternoon; she had finished vacuuming the house and doing her college homework. This free time, which Lily hadn't expected, made her feel anxious as she realized she didn't know what she wanted to do. She was in a mini-crisis, asking herself, "Who am I?"

She realized that everything she wanted and desired over the past few years was based on life with Jack. Lily was convinced that what Jack thought was right, new, important, and valuable. But what about life on her own, as well as her thoughts, beliefs, and values?

The relationship with Jack ruined her sense of self in unexpected ways. She didn't know what she liked, what goals to pursue, or what things were important. These realizations helped her recognize the need to begin regaining her identity.

Lily committed herself to start doing what she once remembered enjoying again, even if it meant doing it alone. Doing things by herself scared her, especially without Jack's guidance by her side, but it was a necessary part of the process. She felt like a little girl lost in the woods without a compass, not knowing where to go.

Without Jack, the only compass she had was her heart. And unfortunately, but not surprisingly, through the trauma of the toxicity, Lily lost touch with her heart. As a result, she needed to embark on a quest to regain trust in herself. To get that process started, she began to pursue activities that made her happy. Or at least showed her a glimmer of joy or well-being. The more she engaged in these activities, the more she felt like herself.

Lily also began to work on accepting and loving herself through the darkness of heartbreak. She practiced self-compassion, reminding herself it was okay to feel lost and take the time she needed to heal. As the feelings came, she allowed herself to be spontaneous, sensitive, absurd, and even confusing to get to know herself better. She laughed out loud in work meetings, admitted her mistakes without shame, sang her favorite songs on the subway, and took impromptu road trips with friends.

Another crucial step was to reclaim the places and activities that reminded her of Jack. Though necessary, it was not one of her initial steps toward healing. For a long time, the mere thought of revisiting those places evoked unbearable pain. However, after some time, her therapist encouraged her to face those memories by creating new ones. The goal was to make those places her own, as an individual, instead of only being associated with Jack.

She returned to the supermarket they used to frequent and found that shopping alone helped her feel stronger. She went to the same restaurants they used to visit, but this time she brought her sister and coworkers to create new memories.

As Lily continued to reconnect with herself, she worked to let go of Jack's memories that were holding her back. The more she challenged herself to define her values, desires, and preferences, the happier she felt without Jack. Self-love and self-discovery were powerful tools for healing and moving forward, and she realized the journey was as rewarding and exciting as the desired destination.

After focused and diligent effort, Lily rediscovered her passions and embraced her identity as a creative, sensitive, spontaneous, and funny person. She learned that her breakup with Jack allowed her to grow and discover new parts of herself.

- How exactly does a sense of identity get ruined?
- What does healing from identity loss look like?
- What actions help one heal from an identity crisis?
- How do self-compassion and self-awareness help rebuild a sense of self?

Identity loss through "perspecticide" is counterintuitive but critical to understanding why toxicity is so traumatic in its effects. Recovering identity through self-compassion and self-awareness is at the core of the long-term healing process.

HOW A TOXIC RELATIONSHIP RUINS YOUR SENSE OF SELF

Step number four in overcoming and healing a toxic relationship is to reclaim our identity. But what is our identity? What does it mean to lose it exactly?

Our society tries to answer this question in many different ways. Some define identity by social status, family background, or culture. Others define it by religion, profession, and emotions, but does that describe who you are? (1)

All of these questions were on Lily's mind Saturday afternoon as she ran out of productive distractions. So who was she when she wasn't obsessing over Jack, doing chores, or studying for her college exams?

Our identity is how we think of or perceive ourselves. The collection of characteristics, traits, and qualities that define us as individuals. It includes our personality, beliefs, values, experiences, and relationships, and it's also none of these things simultaneously. We must always remember that our identity is fluid and can change over time as we grow and develop.

In a toxic relationship with a narcissistic partner, loss of identity is inevitable. Unfortunately, Lily's sense of self became intertwined with Jack's, and she struggled to distinguish her sense of self from his. And that's where the problem existed. She no longer had an individual identity.

The idea of "no me without them and no them without me" was common throughout her relationship with Jack. She felt she could only exist or function with his guidance and opinions. Because of this, Jack's approval and validation strongly influenced not just her actions but her sense of self-worth and identity. As a result, she usually neglected her needs and desires in favor of Jack's, feeling she would never be happy and fulfilled without her relationship with him.

Her identity was not shattered because it was gone. It was simply hidden under Jack's presence and influence. She became so intertwined with Jack that she felt lost, hopeless, and meaningless when he was no longer present in her life. All decisions were previously based on Jack's wishes and happiness as the beacon of light that guided both their actions.

To redefine her identity, it was necessary to untangle it from Jack by exploring and rediscovering her values, interests, unique qualities, and characteristics. But where to start?

At first, it was difficult for Lily to fully understand the extent of her loss of identity until after she was separated from him. Jack's control over her thoughts was so subtle and ingrained that it became challenging for her to function independently. But the concept of "perspecticide" helped her understand it all. (2)

How do Narcissists Use Perspecticide to Steal Identity?

Perspecticide is the psychological manipulation and control in a toxic or emotionally abusive relationship. The abuser controls the victim's beliefs, perceptions, and thoughts until they lose their sense of self. As a result, the victim experiences constant confusion, self-doubt, and a loss of personal autonomy.

This manipulative tactic, like extreme gaslighting, distorted Lily's thoughts, opinions, and feelings. This allowed Jack to have more control over her actions. This was happening subconsciously for her, which was part of why she stayed in the relationship for so long. (2)

Lily was so afraid of being manipulated again after Jack that she began to doubt her interactions with everyone. She couldn't tell if someone was trying to help her in a healthy manner or influence her in an unhealthy, manipulative way. What helped her was defining the tools Jack used to make her only agree with him instead of thinking for herself.

- **Trauma bonding:** This refers to a toxic pattern of behavior with constant arguments, making the victim feel at fault. After this conflictive phase, there are moments when the abuser shows artificial affection or compassion, which creates a bond based on the shared trauma of the relationship. Despite the difficulties, the victim may feel unable to leave due to the intense desire for these occasional displays of love.

- **Cognitive empathy:** This is when the abuser artificially empathizes with you to manipulate and gain control of your thoughts. Lily recalled how Jack had made her feel like he was the only person who understood her childhood struggles. But then would use that sensitive background to show how "damaged" she was when they fought.

- **Imposing worthlessness:** Jack told her she was wrong whenever Lily tried to impose an opinion. Even when it came to personal tastes like music or clothes, Lily was always "wrong," which led her to listen to his opinions for guidance. (2)

Look at the following symptoms to realize if you are suffering from perspecticide:

- **It's hard to talk about yourself** outside of the traits your narcissist gave you.
- **You lack motivation or a clear purpose in life.** You have stopped believing you deserve things.
- **You feel anxious or uncomfortable when your narcissist is not around.** You feel like you'll do or say the wrong thing without their guidance.
- **You feel like a completely different person,** to the point of not recognizing who you were in the past. (2)

If you're suffering from perspecticide, it's not your fault. Becoming aware of the signs is most of the battle. Now you can consciously change these patterns and rebuild your identity. You can free yourself from their grip by becoming aware of them as a step toward healing.

HEALING FROM IDENTITY LOSS AFTER NARCISSISTIC ABUSE

Because Jack slowly shed Lily's identity throughout their long relationship, reclaiming it wasn't an overnight process. When Lily's sense of self was shattered, she felt she could never rebuild it. Fortunately, with the help of her therapist and her determination to heal, she took several important steps to move forward with a stronger sense of self. She could rebuild a more authentic, meaningful, and fulfilling identity by rebuilding self-esteem, increasing self-awareness, clarifying values and goals, and committing to small, meaningful actions.

To do that, she first **surrounded herself with a group of supportive people.** She committed to identifying and not spending time with negative, immature, or draining individuals and hanging out with interesting people who had a positive outlook on life and had nothing but her best intentions at heart.

She cut all the other people out of her life who made her feel bad, guilty, or anxious. This was not easy and often painful, but she understood she needed people to support the new identity she was forging.

Lily also began to **explore new things she liked.** She tried different hobbies and activities, listened to new and exciting music, traveled to nearby cities, and visited new venues with her friends. With kindness and patience, she **wrote about all her experiences in a small journal**, her favorite and not-so-favorite aspects. Lily felt like she was the main character in a new book she was writing, and every day was like a new adventure.

She became comfortable **exploring, defining, and naming the values that were unique about her and important to her,** such as honesty, integrity, compassion, and creativity. Remember that your values are like your personal compass and should guide your decisions and actions in life. (3)

It wasn't easy at first, of course. She had never asked herself these questions before, and it felt like looking into an unknown bottomless pit she was afraid to fill. But as she became more confident, she found the self-discovery process to be a very comforting experience. (4)

Another great piece of advice that helped Lily regain her identity was **doing what Jack convinced her she couldn't do.** For example, Jack never believed she could graduate from college or join a dance class without dropping out after a few weeks.

It was important for Lily to prove to herself that she was capable of those things—and she did. She is now the proud owner of her small fashion boutique and has performed several shows around town with her tap dance group. It wasn't easy at first because Jack's voice in her head kept telling her she was going to fail. But after a few weeks of attending class consistently, she realized her actions were more powerful than the memories of his doubtful taunting. (3)

Lily also worked on **recognizing and finding compassion for her own emotions** and stories. What helped her most in regaining her sense of self was **self-compassion**. Being kind to herself made a huge difference in Lily's mental well-being.

She sought out stories of people who went through similar experiences to remind herself she was not alone, and she committed to not defining herself by her toxic relationship. She also stopped blaming and berating herself for what happened, which helped her feel more solid and confident in her choices. (5)

How to Rebuild Your Self-esteem After Narcissistic Abuse

Self-esteem is the first thing a narcissist erodes to take away identity. If you don't value yourself, it's much easier to be manipulated. This may sound counterintuitive, or perhaps these two topics seem unrelated. However, to improve your self-esteem after narcissistic abuse, it is essential to develop self-awareness.

According to a study by Sati Unal in 2014, working on self-awareness can considerably improve self-esteem. This practice allows you to be more accepting of your personality and better understand your capabilities. Self-awareness means knowing your strengths, weaknesses, and motivations behind your actions.

Lily wanted to change her life after the breakup but realized she didn't know where to start! Her therapist helped her conclude that knowing herself was the only way to move in the right direction. Self-awareness helped her choose a lifestyle aligned with her core values and brought her long-term fulfillment and happiness.

Benjamin Franklin, one of the most famous founders of the United States, understood the importance of values to drive identity and direction in life. He defined 13 values that dictated his daily actions. Values like temperance, moderation, cleanliness, and humility, to name a few. At the end of each day, he would review his values and reflect on his actions to see if anything he did that day drove him *away* from his values. If so, he would put a mark next to that value for the day. He would then do his best to understand the root cause of why he didn't follow the value and resolved to do better the following day. This was the daily practice for a man who understood the importance of values. As I've implemented this same practice, it has become a personal identity self-awareness compass for me. (7)

The practice of self-awareness by living and observing the values that dictate behavior also allowed her to set specific goals for her life that motivated her to wake up each morning. Based on her values, she asked herself, "What do I want to achieve in my career, relationships, health, or personal growth?" Then, she ensured her goals were Specific, Measurable, Achievable, Relevant, and Time-bound (SMART). (8)

With these clear purposes in mind, her confidence grew with each goal she set and reached. Finally, Lily started to see a silver lining to the abuse she endured in her toxic relationship with Jack. The healing from the toxicity allowed her to become more aware of who she was. Without this traumatic experience, she would have likely wandered through life, fulfilling other people's expectations without reaching her true potential.

You can become more self-aware by learning about your dreams, strengths, and weaknesses through the following exercises:

- **Write down your goals and keep track of them:** The first step in becoming self-aware is to write down your short-term or long-term goals. This exercise will help you identify your goals, values, and skills to manifest the life you want and any shortcomings you may encounter.
- **Practice mindfulness:** Mindfulness refers to a mental state of being fully present and having the mind and body engaged in the present moment. When done correctly, mindfulness allows us to have an open and non-judgmental awareness of our thoughts, feelings, physical sensations, and surroundings. Practicing mindfulness daily can give you more awareness to answer important questions about yourself.
- **Seek out new experiences:** Stepping out of your comfort zone can help you become more aware of how you act, think, and feel. It also creates more opportunities to explore new interests, hidden talents, and positive qualities about yourself.

- **Ask for feedback:** Learning more about
  yourself is easier as you understand how others
  see you. Asking people for honest feedback is
  one of the best ways to increase self-awareness.
  Try to take a non-judgmental or critical
  approach to this exercise, and remember that
  constructive criticism is not a personal attack.
- **Challenge your beliefs and identify your core
  values:** Challenging your beliefs allows you to
  determine what motivates your daily decisions
  and behaviors. This allows you to become more
  flexible and realize you can shape and change
  your beliefs based on your values rather than
  outdated biases. Your core values are the
  principles that guide your existence, the things
  you will continue to pursue even if all your
  basic needs are met. When you identify your
  values, you'll always have a compass to follow in
  life. (6) (7)

Lily realized the space left by her breakup was an
amazing opportunity to rebuild herself. Like the most
talented sculptors, Lily figuratively began to slowly
piece together her legs through self-care, self-compassion, and the support of her loved ones. Then she built
her torso and arms by exploring new hobbies and
engaging in exciting and fulfilling activities that Jack

never thought she would do. Finally, she rounded out her face and head by increasing her self-awareness and clarifying her goals and values. Lily was ready to take her newly crafted self to places and people that made her feel fulfilled and aligned with her new identity. Lily was ready to set boundaries and rebuild her world.

MAKE IT STICK

Instructions: As you learned from the chapter above, self-awareness is key to rebuilding identity. Take some time to reflect on the prompts and responses below to increase your self-awareness. Then, answer each question honestly and thoughtfully.

What is your greatest asset or strength? Why? *Use the space provided to expound the answer.*

_____

_____

_____

_____

_____

What are your long-term and short-term goals? Why? *Use the space provided to expound the answer.*

_____

_____

_____

_____

_____

What makes you feel hurt and why? What weaknesses are you working on being compassionate towards yourself about?

_____

_____

_____

_____

_____

What activities or experiences are you interested in trying? Why? *Use the space provided to expound the answer.*

_____

_____

_____

_____

_____

What are your core values that drive your daily actions? *Use the space provided to expound the answer.*

_____

_____

_____

_____

_____

What makes me truly happy and fulfilled and why? *Use the space provided to expound the answer.*

_____

_____

_____

_____

_____

Remember that rebuilding identity is a journey, not a destination. It may take time to figure out who you are, your values, and what you want in life, and that's okay. Be patient and compassionate with yourself as you explore new interests and challenge your limiting beliefs to live in alignment with your authentic self.

8

STEP 5: BOUNDARIES - THE KEY TO REBUILDING YOUR WORLD

"Givers need to set limits because takers rarely do."

— RACHEL WOLCHIN

After several months of separation, Lily made significant progress in her healing journey. She was happy with the new identity she created for herself, with her new routine, job, colleagues, and friendships. But one night before she went to bed, an unknown number popped up on her phone screen. She was hesitant to answer but decided to pick up the phone anyway. When she did, she was met with what her intuition had forewarned her about. It was Jack.

152 | LISANNE MURPHY

However, there was no trace of the confident and self-assured person she remembered Jack to be. Instead, the voice on the other end of the phone was that of a lost, depressed, and desperate person looking for a few crumbs of love.

Lily wanted to be strong and hang up the phone, but Jack's unwavering distressed cry made her stay a little longer to give him some words of comfort.

After that call, Lily didn't hear from Jack for weeks. She almost forgot about the encounter when another unknown number appeared on her phone screen. These calls, in which Jack cried, and Lily comforted him, continued for some time.

But Lily never felt better after Jack hung up the phone. On the one hand, she felt sheepishly triumphant to hear that Jack's shining image of perfection was brought down by his insecurities. But when she started to think about what was bothering her, she discovered that her interactions with Jack were not fulfilling to Lily; they were a yearning for comfort when he felt overwhelmed by his emotions.

Their interactions were still about Jack's life, problems, and needs, never Lily's. He never asked her how she was, and although their relationship dynamic was always like that when they were together, it felt more wrong this time.

She realized once again Jack was taking advantage of her. So the next time he called, Lily told him she didn't want him to call her anymore and that it would be better if they didn't stay in touch. Maybe it was her firm voice, her confident demeanor, or the fact that, for the first time, Lily was putting a boundary on the relationship, but it truly felt like Jack no longer had power over her.

At first, he became more aggressive and demanding. Jack knew exactly what to say and do to get Lily into a fight with him. After all, this is how narcissists like Jack feed their egos and need for attention. Lily, however, didn't take the bait, remained firm in her boundaries, and refused to fall into the traps Jack set for her. As a result, the calls became more sporadic, especially since Lily would only answer the phone if it were someone she knew. And eventually, Jack stopped calling her.

- Why is it important to create boundaries for someone who has been in a toxic relationship?
- What were the biggest obstacles in setting boundaries?
- What role do boundaries play in avoiding being in another toxic relationship?

Setting boundaries with an ex is essential, especially if the ex was a narcissist or had other toxic qualities. Setting boundaries can also help you establish your identity, regain control of your life, and protect yourself from further emotional harm.

BUILDING & MAINTAINING HEALTHY RELATIONSHIPS THROUGH BOUNDARIES

Boundaries are the physical, emotional, and mental limits we set to protect our well-being, maintain our personal identity, and respect our and our partner's autonomy. Setting and respecting boundaries is essential to building and maintaining healthy relationships. It helps to prevent misunderstandings, conflict, and emotional harm, as well as to develop trust and intimacy with our partner. (1)

But for someone who has been in a toxic relationship like Lily, the concept of boundaries sounded foreign. She always felt responsible for Jack's actions and emotions. She stopped doing many enjoyable activities because Jack didn't like coming home and not having her around. She also stopped hanging out with good friends because Jack thought she was too affectionate or close to those other friends.

The lack of boundaries in Lily's relationship was another sign of her low self-esteem and lack of a solid identity that was carved away from her. But there was something that kept Lily attached to her relationship. The two were on a constant rollercoaster of intense emotions, where every problem felt like a train wreck, followed by equally dramatic romantic makeup. This cycle of volatility, followed by rescue, accomplished Jack's goal of manipulating and taking advantage of her.

Sometimes Jack would elicit feelings of bliss and euphoria, and other times she would be torn and unable to make a simple decision without bursting into tears. This is the dynamic of toxic and codependent relationships without clear boundaries. (2)

The Challenge of Establishing Boundaries After a Toxic Relationship

The lack of boundaries directly relates to codependency. People who desperately need the love and affection of others are unable to set clear boundaries because they are too afraid of rejection. As a result, they sacrifice their needs and, ultimately, their identity to receive love from their partner.

Lily unnecessarily took responsibility for Jack's emotions, decisions, and actions, known as a **savior**

personality type. She was on a never-ending quest to save and fix him with unconditional love and understanding. In return, she hoped Jack would reward her with the love, affirmation, and affection she always wanted. But usually, Jack always played the victim, making Lily feel accountable for his feelings and actions. It was Lily's fault he felt lonely in the evenings if she decided to go to music or dance lessons. It was Lily's fault Jack felt jealous when she spent too much time with her friends.

These two types of people, the savior and the victim, are attracted to each other without ever being able to meet each other's emotional needs. They perpetuate the low self-esteem and codependency entanglement that keeps them in a toxic relationship.

Jack was constantly creating problems to feel like a victim and to be rescued by Lily. Deep down, this was a flawed strategy to feel loved. In the same way, Lily tried to save Jack, not because she truly cared about his problem, but also to make herself feel deserving of love. Unfortunately, both tactics resulted in no healthy forms of love, just codependency.

For someone like Jack, the hardest thing to do is take responsibility for his feelings and actions. After all, people with narcissistic tendencies believe they must blame others to elevate their ego to be worthy of being loved and wanted. Letting go of this belief threatens the only way they think they know how to obtain affection, which is terrifying. In Lily's case, encouraging Jack or anyone else she liked to take responsibility for their own choices without fixing their problems also threatens the only way she thought she could be loved, which was to step in, overserve, and try to save Jack from his pain. (2)

It was only when Lily began rebuilding her self-esteem that she understood how the vicious and poisonous cycle of trying to gain love and affection by taking responsibility for Jack's emotions and actions occurred. And most importantly, how to set clear boundaries to avoid falling back into the venom.

HOW TO CREATE HEALTHY BOUNDARIES IN ROMANTIC RELATIONSHIPS

We live in a culture and society that rewards self-sacrifice for the common good. But unfortunately, this can lead to the mistaken belief that we must always say yes to every request and try to please everyone. As a result, many people sabotage their well-being to avoid rejection or make someone else happy. The deeper consequence of this systemic lack of boundaries is low self-esteem.

If poor boundaries reflect low self-esteem, Lily's course was to build her sense of worth by setting healthy boundaries in her relationships. As we described earlier in the book, self-esteem is not a prize you magically get after a lot of effort, and merely thinking about it is equally not helpful. Self-esteem is the natural by-product of self-aware, well-adjusted people, and it comes after you look at your own life experiences with self-compassion. Notice that boundaries always come back to self-awareness. Don't underestimate the power of being self-aware.

Don't be discouraged by realizing you may have low self-esteem. Everyone struggles with something, even the wealthiest, most attractive, most famous people in the world. This statement isn't something I'm saying to make you feel better; it's a fact. Unfortunately, people with low self-esteem think they're worse than everyone else, which is a cognitive bias that doesn't match objective reality.

After some enlightening therapy sessions, Lily realized she was constantly putting herself down, unable to recognize her talents and skills, and focused too much on her weaknesses. So she made a balanced list of the positive and less favorable aspects of her character to have a more objective outlook on her personality. This exercise helped her accept her flaws, become more confident in her strengths, and ultimately become more comfortable in her own skin.

Working on her shortcomings no longer felt like a constant reminder of her imperfections but an inspiring exercise that helped her to know herself better. Ironically, accepting herself in the present, rather than waiting to be more intelligent, funnier, or prettier, after working hard on herself, inspired her to work harder, and her self-esteem improved more quickly and naturally.

As she often told her friends, it didn't happen overnight. It took patience, time, and effort on Lily's part, and some days were better than others. However, she ended up in a much better place than even before her relationship with Jack. Setting boundaries felt like a natural part of life instead of a challenging, jaw-clenching guilt trip she could never sustain.

Lily's intuition became sharp and active, always ready to tell her how she was feeling and what behaviors she could and could not tolerate from others. Before saying yes to any plan or favor someone else asked of her, she checked in with herself and asked, "Do I really want to do this?"

Her gut instinct usually won the day. She allowed herself to honor those feelings if the answer was a resounding NO. At first, it felt uncomfortable to disappoint others, but it felt worse to put her own well-being at risk. And she learned that her true friends accepted her decisions regardless of what they were.

Since she realized boundaries were necessary for her mental well-being, Lily respectfully removed herself from environments that didn't energize her, distanced herself from people who didn't validate her feelings, and prioritized her wants and needs over other people's demands.

Like Lily, you can set and reinforce your boundaries, even if you don't feel your self-esteem is as high as you'd like. The following tips will make the process easier. (2)

- **Literally set boundaries:** Defining your boundaries may be easier said than done, but it's the only way to reinforce them and protect your overall well-being. What behavior, people, or treatment are you unwilling to tolerate? You can define your boundaries in every situation and relationship in your life, whether at work, on a date, or even with your family.

- **Decide the consequences if someone oversteps your boundaries:** Now that you've defined your boundaries, determine the consequences. You may need to change the consequences depending on the situation, person, or context, so it's best to define them as early as possible.

- **Communicate your boundaries and the consequences clearly:** The next step is to let other people know the above, especially those closest to you. This will prevent many conflicts and disagreements and ensure a positive environment that protects your well-being. Ensure that those you are communicating with can repeat to you what the boundary is and how it will help the relationship. It's often surprising to realize what we feel we communicate and what is actually heard are often quite different.

- **Be firm in enforcing the consequences of your boundaries:** It's helpful if done in a spirit of love and understanding. The boundary is meant to help both partners feel safe and understood. It may be uncomfortable initially, but if someone crosses your boundaries, walk away to cool down or do what you say you'll do. Your well-being is worth it. But, on the other hand, don't break your boundaries by not following through on the consequences. They are only boundaries if they stay boundaries.

SETTING BOUNDARIES WITH A NARCISSISTIC EX-PARTNER

Ideally, people should respect our boundaries if we communicate them. However, narcissistic, toxic partners or ex-partners will always look for ways to overstep them and have control over you, as that is the previously established pattern. Setting boundaries means a change of routine. They can't manipulate you because they don't have control over you anymore, which is what narcissistic people fear and fight most. (3)

Setting boundaries after a breakup is essential to healing from the relationship, protecting your emotional and psychological well-being, and even safe-guarding yourself from dangerous situations.

The following are common interactions and conversations that Lily and Jack had on a daily basis that show how he violated boundaries:

- "No, you can't go out with Aaron because I'll get jealous. I don't care if he is just your friend. He acts suspicious. So don't hang out with others if I'm not around."
- "If you want me to forgive you, block all the men you've spoken to in the past. You know I don't like to feel insecure."
- "I don't understand why you're so angry that I showed up unannounced. I just wanted to surprise you."
- "Why won't you let me handle that situation for you? I just want to help, and I know I can do it better than you can." (4)

At first, setting boundaries with a toxic partner can feel impossible, especially if *no contact* is off the table (for example, if you are co-parenting children). After all, toxic or narcissistic ex-partners don't react well to boundaries, and you may know they won't respect them.

If you would like to review more tips on how to co-parent with a narcissistic ex-partner, I invite you to follow this link to read the additional BONUS chapter created exclusively for readers of this book. www.heal ingtoxicity.com/breathe-again-bonus

The most important thing to acknowledge is that you can never do enough to make your narcissistic ex happy. So instead of prioritizing their feelings, put your needs at the forefront of all your decisions. Don't be afraid to set firm boundaries, even if you think your toxic ex won't comply.

Remember, your narcissistic ex will do anything to control and manipulate you to feed their ego. They believe they have unrestricted access to all areas of your life and can decide how to treat you. Don't be discouraged. Standing firm in your boundaries means they no longer have power over you. They will get the message over time. (5)

Once you've established your boundaries, the consequences of crossing them, and communicated them to your ex, use the following strategies:

- **Don't take the bait:** Your ex knows precisely what to say or do to manipulate you. They will try to bait you into a conflict or fight to get your attention. List all the baits you can think of before you meet with them. It's hard not to take the bait initially, but you'll get there with practice and conscious effort.

- **Get ahead of their patterns:** If you keep in touch with your ex, you'll notice specific behavior patterns. For example, they may accuse you of doing something ridiculous every two or three weeks or verbally attack you out of the blue. Anticipating these behaviors will help you respond in the way you want to. In addition, writing down these interactions to find the pattern can be helpful. For example, if your ex says X, you will respond with Y. This will help you get ahead of them and regain your power.

- **Don't explain yourself:** You don't need to explain or justify your boundaries to your ex. Besides, explaining to them won't make them stop or change how they act or perceive you. So get used to expressing your boundaries and the consequences of crossing them without further explanation. This will prove that you are confident and don't need their permission to act.

- **Withhold personal details about your life:** Be aloof and impersonal when you see your ex, and don't show any interest in their personal life. Don't worry about being rude or disrespectful! Instead, save your personal details for someone who really deserves to hear them and cares about you. Besides, if they don't know anything about your personal life, they won't have material to bring you into conflict or share their unwanted opinions.

- **Don't apologize:** Remind yourself every day that you didn't do anything wrong! There's no reason to apologize to your narcissistic ex-partner. Apologizing will only feed their ego, so just don't do it. You are not responsible for their feelings or actions, so stand your ground.

- **Don't take things personally:** One of the most complex parts of setting boundaries with your narcissistic ex is not taking things personally. It hurts when your ex says hurtful things about you because they know your weaknesses and vulnerabilities. Narcissistic people bully others to feed their ego, so remember that before taking things personally. Most importantly, it also shows they don't have power over you.

- **Communicate via text:** Finally, try to communicate only by text or writing; if it's email, even better. This will make your boundaries even more straightforward, and you'll be able to express them in a way that leaves no room for misinterpretation. You'll also have more control over your reactions and be less likely to take their bait. (5)

Setting firm boundaries will help you deal with your narcissistic ex-partner and prevent you from returning to a toxic relationship. Once you master these strategies, you'll find that your world has been rebuilt in a more healthy way.

5 Tips for Avoiding Another Toxic Relationship

Lily realized the main reason she hadn't wanted to date for a long time, outside of focusing on her healing, was the fear of returning to the same toxic cycle. Once she expressed that concern to her therapist, she offered Lily 5 tips to break the repetitive dynamics of unhealthy toxic relationships.

After following them, she felt like she could walk out of her house with her head up, open to the next adventures and interactions, knowing the power to create the world she wanted to experience was within her.

1. Do a relationship inventory: This step involves examining all your relationships to see common denominators and identify patterns. This exercise sheds light on behaviors and choices you weren't aware of before. A relationship inventory also helps you determine what you find attractive or valuable in a romantic partner or relationship and what things you shy away from.

When doing your relationship inventory for a relationship that has ended, answer the following questions:

- Why did the relationship end?
- What did I do to cause the relationship to end?
- What did I like and dislike about this person?

Then, create three columns with the following information:

- What are my must-haves and deal-breakers in a relationship?
- What things can I be flexible about?
- What things do I not care about?

This exercise will help you set healthy boundaries and recognize the red flags when meeting new people or starting a new relationship.

2. Look at your patterns: We unconsciously make the same choices and follow the same patterns without realizing it. It has to do with past experiences and the beliefs that shape our world and reality.

To avoid making unconscious choices, ask yourself the following questions:

- What types of people do I tend to date?
- What are the characteristics of the relationships I always end up in?
- What causes conflict in my relationships?
- What is my role in the problems of my relationships?

3. Look at what thoughts and feelings influence your decisions: If you find yourself dating the same type of person repeatedly, look at what's happening inside you.

To increase your self-awareness, ask yourself the following questions:

- How does this person make you feel right now?
- What thoughts come to mind when you start dating?
- How do they relate to your core beliefs about relationships?

For example, if you believe you are not good enough for a lasting relationship, this thought may drive you to date emotionally unavailable people. Once you clarify the core belief causing your actions, you can test the belief in real-life situations.

Let's dig into this scenario more in-depth as someone who's become aware of a tendency to date emotionally unavailable people. You might try dating someone specifically looking for an established relationship, taking things slowly when dating, and doing the work of getting to know each other on an intimate level instead of bolting or sabotaging at the first signs of commitment.

How does your core belief play out in this situation? This can help you live life not defined by core beliefs and create evidence for alternative thinking and new beliefs.

4. Explore what kind of person you are attracting: We tend to attract people with the same emotional development state as we are. If you continue to attract emotionally unavailable people, it may be time to take a break and work on your own emotional unavailability. As you progress on your self-development journey, you'll naturally attract more emotionally mature people.

5. Know your attachment style: Finally, knowing your attachment style will shed light on why you keep attracting the same people and how you can break out of this cycle. As mentioned in previous chapters, people with an anxious attachment style tend to have codependent relationships, and people with an avoidant attachment style have difficulty forming intimate and close relationships. Identify your attachment style and start working on adapting it as needed. (6)

Once Lily worked on her self-esteem and felt more comfortable in her skin, she could set healthy boundaries in every environment and relationship. Saying yes to Jack's demands was more manageable than she once thought. While setting boundaries, she learned a lot about herself, the things she was flexible about, and the behaviors she was unwilling to tolerate from others. It wasn't easy to define her deal breakers and must-haves, but doing so helped her reshape her world in a healthy and inspiring way. For once, Lily didn't feel her choices were out of her control. The dating scene was no longer a dark place filled with threats and hazards but a fulfilling place where she could live her life to the fullest and find meaningful connections.

MAKE IT STICK

Instructions: Four boundary types are essential for maintaining a healthy relationship:

1. Physical Boundaries: These boundaries refer to physical touch, personal space, and sexual boundaries. This includes handshakes, hugs, and intimate physical contact.

2. Emotional Boundaries: These are related to our feelings and emotions. It refers to our ability to express our feelings and set limits on how much we are willing to share with others.

3. Intellectual Boundaries: These boundaries are associated with our thoughts and beliefs. It refers to our ability to express our opinions and respect the views of others.

4. Spiritual Boundaries: These speak of our core values and beliefs. It represents our ability to express our spirituality and respect the beliefs of others.

Take some time to reflect on the prompts and responses below to reflect on your boundaries. Then, answer each question honestly and thoughtfully.

Do you feel comfortable communicating your physical boundary needs? Can you ask for what you want and need without feeling bad? *Use the space provided to expound the answer.*

_____

_____

_____

_____

_____

Are you comfortable with the level of emotional intimacy in your relationships? Are there certain emotions that you find difficult to express? *Use the space provided to expound the answer.*

_____

_____

_____

_____

_____

Do you acknowledge and respect other people's opinions, even if you disagree with them? *Use the space provided to expound the answer.*

_____

_____

_____

_____

Do you feel comfortable expressing your opinions and beliefs in your relationships? *Use the space provided to expound the answer.*

_____

_____

_____

_____

_____

Are you able to recognize when others are crossing your boundaries? How do you respond in these situations? *Use the space provided to expound the answer.*

_____

_____

_____

_____

_____

Do you feel like those around you respect and acknowledge your spiritual beliefs? *Use the space provided to expound the answer.*

_____

_____

_____

_____

_____

Remember that setting boundaries doesn't prevent you from having fulfilling relationships. If someone doesn't accept your boundaries, the person is not for you. The more you recognize and reinforce your boundaries, the more you'll surround yourself with people who respect your boundaries and truly care about your well-being and happiness.

9

THE 5 STEPS IN ACTION: A COMPREHENSIVE FRAMEWORK FOR HEALING

> *"Healing is the return of the memory of whole-ness. When the body, mind, and spirit work together, anything is possible."*
>
> — DEEPAK CHOPRA

The five steps explored in the previous chapters can help you understand and organize the healing process after leaving a toxic relationship. Still, it's important to note that there is no specific timeline for healing. For example, Lily sometimes felt like a failure when she woke up with a heavy heart and tears in her eyes several months after the breakup. Some days she felt confident, able to communicate and reinforce her boundaries, and ready to meet new people.

On other days, however, the memories of Jack, his absence, and the trauma from the toxicity felt almost unbearable.

She wanted to follow a linear process and feel better each day. When she shared this desire with her therapist, her therapist encouraged Lily to shift her perspective. Lily realized that forcing herself to feel better after breaking up with Jack was detrimental to her inner work. Lily cruelly judged her feelings, flaws, and weaknesses and wondered why she couldn't just "get over him." A constant reminder was needed to accept the situation, be present with her feelings, and patiently work through the emotions as they surfaced.

She needed to take things one day at a time, embrace her pain (Step 1), and use it as an opportunity for introspection. By allowing herself to feel the pain and explore the root causes of her emotions, Lily was able to learn about her struggles in a non-judgmental way. As a result, she began to see her worth and realized that her feelings and experiences, even the most painful ones, did not determine her value (Step 2).

With a more robust self-awareness (Step 4), Lily continued cultivating self-love and self-compassion in her daily life (Step 2). She learned that part of loving herself was making room for uncomfortable feelings and thoughts without beating herself up (Step 1). She also leaned on her friends and family for support without feeling like a burden, and she trusted her therapist's guidance as she worked through her trauma (Step 3).

As Lily prioritized her well-being, she found she could say no to things that didn't enrich her life. Setting boundaries and prioritizing her needs became a natural exercise that empowered her to take control of her life and relationships (Step 5).

These steps worked together as a cycle, and they sometimes happened simultaneously. For example, Lily would feel depressed and unsure at times yet still practiced self-love and self-compassion. Sometimes she felt lost and lacked self-confidence, but she practiced self-awareness to speed up the healing process.

Slowly but surely, Lily began to heal from the pain of her ended toxic relationship. She found happiness and fulfillment in her life and eventually built healthy relationships based on mutual respect and trust. Looking back on her journey, Lily realized the more she truly knows who she is and how she responds to life's ups and downs, the better she can navigate challenges when they come her way.

- How did Lily experiencing the 5 Steps help to recover and heal from her toxic relationship?
- Did she go through each step separately or experience them simultaneously?
- How did Lily work on multiple steps at the same time?

The 5 Steps of Healing and Overcoming your toxic relationship are not necessarily linear, nor are they stepping stones or levels you must "pass" to move forward in the game. The 5 Steps are a cycle. Learning strategies for working on multiple steps simultaneously will be valuable to your healing journey.

THE 5 STEPS TO HEALING ARE A CYCLE

The 5 Steps to healing we explored, discussed, and understood in the previous chapters do not necessarily follow a linear progression. Getting started in a linear fashion can help you approach them in a more organized way. However, you can work on them simultaneously until you are more fully healed. You may also need to revisit them occasionally as life throws curve balls.

TOXIC RELATIONSHIPS: BREATHE AGAIN | 181

Step 1: Allowing Yourself to Feel the Pain

Step 2: Strengthening the Inner Self Through Forgiveness and Self-Love

Step 3: Seeking Support from Professionals in Healing

Step 4: Reclaiming Your Identity in the Aftermath of a Toxic Relationship

Step 5: Boundaries - The Key To Rebuilding Your World

How the 5 Steps Work Together

Rather than shying away from the fear, grief, anxiety, and sadness that remains after a breakup, you can kindly make room for these feelings to emerge in a non-judgmental way. It's difficult to be in the middle of this whirlwind of emotions, and it certainly doesn't seem like something to celebrate, but accepting the feelings is honestly the fastest way out. As a result, your self-awareness will improve, and you can better recognize and understand your thoughts, feelings, and behaviors.

At the same time, a strong sense of self leads you to cultivate self-love and self-compassion in every decision you make. Part of loving yourself is being willing to ask for help because asking for help is also helping yourself. This choice means you prioritize your well-being, which also empowers you to say no to things that don't bring joy or value to your life. In this way, you will eventually move forward, become happy and whole, and be able to build healthy relationships from there.

Now seeing how the five steps work together, here are some helpful examples for combining them on your journey to healing and recovery.

HOW TO WORK ON MULTIPLE STEPS AT THE SAME TIME

Combining the steps to aid the healing will help you holistically approach the process. To do this, think about which step you are struggling with and see if combining it with another step might help get you out of the rut you are finding yourself in.

How to Practice Self-Love (Step 2) While Coping with Pain (Step 1)

When we live with pain, especially after a breakup, we sometimes feel it's impossible to escape it and enjoy life. We wake up with the nagging pain in the background, go about our day with it lurking behind our shoulders, eat with it hanging over our heads, have social interactions that seem muted or meaningless, and then go to sleep and are often haunted by our pain in our dreams.

Lily sometimes felt like no matter how much therapy and work she did to heal. The pain would always creep back in.

She often blamed herself for not trying hard enough or "doing healing better." But unfortunately, that mindset was not the key to working through the pain. We certainly don't want to experience uncomfortable emotions, but fighting them and blaming ourselves for their existence only adds a harmful shame cycle to the already devastating heartbreak and trauma recovery.

Lily realized the most helpful thing she could do to support her healing journey was to move away from guilt, anger, and resentment and find ways to renew her sense of purpose even when the pain was there. Instead of fighting these emotions, she made room for them through self-love and self-compassion. She allowed the pain and acceptance of self-love to coexist.

She practiced self-compassion by being gentler, kinder, and more understanding with herself, especially during the most painful times. As a result, she got enough rest, reduced her to-do list, asked for support when needed, and trusted her healing process.

This shift in her mindset made her realize that pain was not the enemy. Instead, it was a sign that her body, mind, and heart were trying to heal. The less she

184 | LISANNE MURPHY

resisted the pain, the faster the pain was integrated and released. She also realized she could still experience the joys of life between the waves of pain and grief. So she created happiness in the small things, like making her favorite food, watching her favorite movies, and spending time with friends during the most challenging days.

In this way, Lily slowly realized that pain wasn't a punishment to endure. Loving herself through the pain made the road to healing easier and less overwhelming. (1)

The Benefits of Seeking Professional Help (Step 3) When Reclaiming Your Identity (Step 4)

As mentioned in Chapter 7, self-awareness refers to the way we perceive our personality and the characteristics that define our identity and drive our behavior. Knowing our likes, dislikes, personality traits, and core values allows us to develop fulfilling relationships and set purposeful goals to pursue a worthwhile life.

Defining and reclaiming identity can be overwhelming if you've never considered it. But unfortunately, many spend life trying to fulfill other people's desires and expectations, so getting stuck in the process of increasing self-awareness is common.

A mental health professional can help identify your values, uncover attachment issues or problematic patterns, and teach techniques to improve decision-making skills. Your therapist can also help you manage symptoms of anxiety or depression related to your sense of self and encourage you to set clear goals to help you pursue your values and interests. (2)

The Power of Asking for Help (Step 3) When Coping With Pain (Step 1)

A breakup can turn your whole world upside down from one moment to the next, making it one of the most stressful experiences in life. A separation from a toxic relationship compounds the difficulty. It triggers challenging, painful, and unsettling emotions and takes us into uncharted territory from one moment to the next, leaving us feeling completely vulnerable.

Asking for help is critical during this difficult and confusing time. Feeling alone and isolating yourself from the rest of the world can sabotage the healing process. Don't try to experience this alone; ask your loved ones for support.

Spending time with people who have gone through painful breakups can be very comforting. They will empathize with your pain, give you valuable advice, and remind you that there's a light at the end of the tunnel.

Choose people who are supportive and uplifting. Surround yourself with positive people who listen to you and encourage you to be authentic without making you feel guilty. And if asking your loved ones for help is not enough, find a therapist you are comfortable opening up with. Make it a priority to find a place to express your feelings and needs safely. (3)

SETTING BOUNDARIES WITH YOUR EX (STEP 5) WHILE...

Strengthening the Inner Self Through Self-Love (Step 2)

Boundaries are a natural extension of practicing self-love. The more we take care of ourselves and honor our wants and needs, the more we'll be willing to set boundaries and communicate them without feeling guilty. For example, Lily demonstrated how she wanted to be treated when she told Jack what was acceptable and unacceptable.

Setting boundaries also helped her not force listening to Jack and comforting him when she didn't want to. Self-love and self-care allowed her to define and strengthen her boundaries. Setting boundaries allowed her to cultivate self-love and self-care in her healing journey.

Reclaiming Your Identity (Step 4)

Setting boundaries also comes naturally as you reclaim your identity. If you don't know who you are, what you like, and what your core values and goals are in life, then you won't know what exactly you're willing and not willing to tolerate from others.

Boundaries express your authentic self because they allow you to separate yourself from those around you. This will create interdependence in your relationships instead of unhealthy codependence where boundaries are lacking. Creating boundaries defines your choices and helps you see why they differ from your ex's.

Setting boundaries helped Lily separate her identity from Jack's expectations and manipulative control. Finally, Lily was free to have personal choices, opinions, and preferences. She had her own thoughts and feelings and didn't need Jack or anyone else to make her feel whole again.

Moving on From Emotional Pain (Step 1)

Boundaries are also a great way to prevent your ex from doing more emotional damage and exacerbating the pain you are already dealing with. All breakups are painful and challenging, and navigating them in a safe environment with people who support you is essential to moving on from the emotional pain.

For this reason, setting boundaries will also keep you safe and prevent you from falling back into the lies and manipulations your toxic ex-partner will try to play on you. (4)

Why Developing a Strong Sense of Self (Step 4) is Crucial for Navigating Pain (Step 1)

As a last example, rebuilding your identity and developing a strong sense of self can help you navigate the pain associated with your breakup. The more you truly know yourself and how you respond to your environment and experiences, the better you can navigate pain and grief.

The grieving process requires us to feel things, no matter how much we try to avoid the experience. Once we feel the pain, we'll see what we need to get back on track. Lily's breakup was a valuable opportunity to learn more about herself, and she now knows how to take care of herself when the inevitable life problems come her way. Self-awareness and pain management work together for healing. (5)

Lily created her authentic healing journey by working through the 5 Steps as a cycle. She found a way to express her unique essence as she went through the life-changing process of recovering from one of her life's most traumatic yet somehow enriching experiences: breaking up with Jack. Your healing journey doesn't have to look like anyone else's; however, the steps are universal principles that will work for anyone recovering from a traumatic breakup. Tailor the cycle to your needs and feelings, and learn to work through each step as a cycle.

MAKE IT STICK

Instructions: Take some time to reflect on the prompts and responses below to identify your emotions and help you work through the 5 Steps.

How do you feel today? What emotions do you recognize? On a scale of zero to 10, how strong are these emotions? (Step 1) *Use the space provided to expound the answer.*

_____

_____

_____

_____

_____

Why do you think you feel this way today? (Step 4) *Use the space provided to expound the answer.*

_____

_____

_____

_____

_____

Who can you talk to when you feel this way? (Step 3) *Use the space provided to expound the answer.*

_____

_____

_____

_____

_____

What helps you feel a little better when you feel like this? (Step 2) *Use the space provided to expound the answer.*

_____

_____

_____

_____

_____

This intense emotion indicates that something important to you is in play. What do you think it is? (Step 4) *Use the space provided to expound the answer.*

_____

_____

_____

_____

_____

What can you do to protect yourself while feeling vulnerable? How can you express those needs? *(Step 5)* *Use the space provided to expound the answer.*

_____

_____

_____

_____

_____

Remember that pain is a part of life. Trying to fight it or avoid it is not only futile; it's what makes pain so over-whelming. So instead of fighting the pain, treat it with compassion, use it to learn more about yourself, set clear boundaries, and discover how to work with it the next time it comes.

10

STAYING ON TRACK: HOW TO HANDLE RELAPSE IN A TOXIC RELATIONSHIP

> *"A bad relationship is like standing on broken glass; if you stay, you will keep hurting. If you walk away, you will hurt, but eventually, you will heal."*

— AUTUMN KOHLER

When Lily was feeling well, it was clear for her to see the damaging impact of her toxic relationship with Jack on her self-esteem, identity, and confidence. Lily truly felt hatred for the entire relationship. She resented the day she met Jack, how he never let her go out with her friends, how she spent hours crying on the bathroom floor, overwhelmed with fear and anxiety when he left the house and wouldn't answer his phone.

Lily went out to meet new people to reinforce the desired separation from him, made weekend plans with her classmates, and talked about coffee roasts with the cute barista at her favorite coffee shop.

But all that faded away on other days when she woke up and missed Jack. She missed the cheesy good morning texts she woke up to every morning, the love notes and surprise flowers he gave her when he picked her up from her college classes, and the sleepless nights they spent talking and cuddling when they started dating.

At the core of her feelings was the desire to have him understand all the damage she had endured and how much he hurt her.

She fantasized about Jack begging for forgiveness and holding her in a long, heartfelt hug that would erase all the bad things that happened. Imagining everything would be okay from now on. In this idealized dream state, Jack and Lily would make up and continue their relationship like the fairy tale it was when they first met.

Logically, Lily knew she could meet someone new and fall in love again. Someone who was emotionally mature worked on their self-awareness and could give her a healthy and fulfilling relationship. In short, someone who truly loved and wanted the best for her. But sometimes the pain was so much that she couldn't help it if her heart still longed for Jack.

The nature of Jack and Lily's relationship created irreparable damage. Choosing to stay away from her toxic ex was not an easy choice. However, she patiently went through the 5 Steps of Healing and Recovery and consciously tried to cut ties with Jack and remove him from her life. And not just because the relationship was toxic but because she became a new and different person through her healing journey. She had to remind herself she wasn't the same Lily who had met Jack. Going back was impossible, even though her heart sometimes yearned for it.

Lily understood the pain she was feeling was a natural part of the healing process. So instead of looking for Jack to save her from her pain, she learned to feel the pain and process her emotions without necessarily acting on them. She learned to wait with kindness and compassion for herself until they gently went away.

The support and guidance she received from her therapist and support network allowed her to stay focused on her goal of healing from this toxic relationship, even on bad days. When she felt sad and nostalgic, Lily tried to explore new activities and get to know herself better and used self-love to fill the space in her heart left by Jack. She committed to loving herself and respecting her emotional needs, no matter what. It was a slow process, but Lily overcame the pain and reclaimed her life.

- Why is there such a strong pull to return to a toxic relationship?
- How did she avoid falling back into that relationship?
- Why was getting back together with Jack a bad idea?

The key to not falling back into the same unhealthy relationship and how to prevent yourself from getting sucked back into the toxicity comes down to an awareness of why and how it may happen.

WHY YOU MAY FALL BACK INTO THE SAME TOXIC RELATIONSHIP?

Although Lily's mind knew how bad it would be to return to her relationship with Jack, a part of her heart still held out hope that something would change in him, there are good times and memories to hold on to. The positive memories might even spark a desire to resume the relationship once it's over. (1)

Understanding why you may want to get back together with your ex can motivate you to move away from that decision.

- **It feels familiar and safe:** We live in a fast-paced world that is constantly changing and leaving behind those who can't keep up. According to a National Institute of Mental Health study, an estimated 19.1% of U.S. adults have an anxiety disorder, and the numbers are increasing over time. Relationships create a comfort zone that provides safety, security, and reassurance. So it's perfectly understandable to try to regain that same comforting feeling we lost after the breakup, even if it's filled with problems and toxicity.
- **Seeking constant approval and validation is a priority:** Another reason you may want to get back together with your ex is if you are used to looking to outside influences for happiness and validation. Seeking a partner who gives you a sense of love, accomplishment, and worth based on their words is deeply tempting. Lily got used to Jack telling her what to wear, who to hang out with, and how to act, and he validated her.

With Jack's absence, who would give her a gold star that she's doing things "right"? It's easier to go into a mediocre KNOWN situation than to venture into the UNKNOWN for something that "might" be better.

- **Starting over is daunting and overwhelming:** Starting over can be a very challenging experience that can sometimes be discouraging. This may lead you to believe that getting back together with your ex is easier than starting a new relationship or creating a new routine. However, the emotional labor involved in rebuilding your life is never as draining as returning to a harmful toxic relationship.

- **Holding onto unrealistic ideas of love and relationships:** You've endured abuse for so long because a part of you truly loves or has loved your partner, which is why you justify their demeanor. At the same time, if you have a problematic vision or idea of love, you may be tempted to return to a relationship filled with misery and suffering simply because you think that's all you can get out of any relationship. Attending therapy and challenging your limiting beliefs is critical to your healing process.

- **Deep-seated feelings of inadequacy and insecurity:** One of the most common reasons to want to get back with an ex is that you are dealing with low self-esteem and self-worth. Codependency, the inability to emotionally stand on your own two feet, will keep you in a bad relationship. Insecurities prevent you from finding the strength to stand up for yourself and be on your own. Cultivating self-love as you rebuild your confidence and identity is essential to avoid falling back into the trap of getting back with your toxic ex. (2)

It's important to understand that leaving a toxic relationship is not easy, and it may take time and several attempts to break free. Don't shame or blame yourself if you are struggling with this decision. Instead, practice self-compassion that wherever you are in the healing process is okay and valid based on your current values and beliefs. This, too, is all part of the healing process. With patience, persistence, and the proper support, you'll feel motivated to start building a better future for yourself. You deserve to be in a healthy and loving relationship, and it's okay to take the time you need to heal and recover from the trauma you've experienced. (3)

Exploring the reasons behind a sudden urge to get back with your toxic ex-partner helps you to shy away from the idea and recognize the damage that could happen if you resume the relationship.

WHY REKINDLING A RELATIONSHIP WITH YOUR TOXIC EX IS A BAD IDEA

Most couples who get back together after a massive breakup end up repeating the same mistakes and reliving the same traumas that drove them apart in the first place. Overall, getting back with your ex will prolong the emotional trauma you've already gone through.

The breakup happened for a reason, no matter who initiated it. Returning to your toxic ex could mean not prioritizing the happiness and inner peace you deserve. If you go back into the relationship hoping things will be different, chances are you will be disappointed. Before you know it, you'll be back in the same problematic cycles and behaviors, realizing that some things just don't change. If they did, they would have been resolved when you were together in the first place.

In addition, getting back together with your ex could make them feel like they have control over you again. This decision could lead to this person taking you for granted and putting you through the same pain you experienced in the past. Trying to make things work again requires a lot of emotional energy and effort, which could jeopardize your psychological well-being if both parties aren't all in on radical change (which is often the case). (4)

This reality caused Lily to change her perspective and abandon any thought or effort of returning to Jack. However, the memories of the relationship sometimes seemed to linger in her mind much longer than she had hoped for. Fortunately, her therapist helped her with some valuable tips on how to keep these thoughts from getting in the way of becoming the best version of herself.

How to Stop Thinking About Your Ex

Victims of narcissistic abuse tend to ruminate about their toxic relationship and ex long after the breakup. Rumination refers to the tendency to repeatedly dwell on negative thoughts, regrets, or experiences leading to feeling stuck and unable to move on.

Re-educating herself and learning what a healthy relationship looks like was the first step that helped Lily stop thinking about Jack. Next, she became aware of the beliefs used to justify, rationalize, and normalize the abusive behavior in her toxic relationship. In Lily's case, Jack treated her like the most special person in the world at the beginning of the relationship, making her feel lucky to have found him.

When things changed, Lily couldn't accept the fact that the prince charming she put her trust and hopes in was being abusive. She began to justify and rationalize his behavior. For example, she sometimes told herself that he was like that because of what happened to his parents, his boss was too strict, or she wasn't doing enough to make him happy. Therefore, she believed she was in a normal relationship, and they were just going through a "rough patch."

By re-educating herself and learning about healthy and unhealthy relationship dynamics, Lily slowly detached herself from any happy thoughts that might remain of her relationship with Jack. She recognized that the relationship played its role in her life, but it was time to move on and create new experiences from a fresh, clean slate.

Another exercise that helped her stop thinking about him was to overcome the limitations he created in her life by rebuilding her self-esteem and redefining her values and preferences, as we explained in Step 4 of this book. Lily then began to set daily achievable goals that aligned with these values. At first, her goals focused on her safety to avoid returning to the abusive relationship. Then she focused them on rebuilding her identity and her life direction.

These valuable recommendations allowed Lily to keep busy and accept that she deserved a happier and more fulfilling life. (5)

It's important to note that it's normal to think about your ex occasionally and remember the joyful and painful experiences. Don't beat yourself up or feel like a failure when memories and feelings happen. Instead, allow them to enter your mind and body without fighting or rationalizing them. Notice each thought as it comes and then let it go gently, without judgment, like a cloud moving across the sky and disappearing into the distance.

If the thoughts are too overwhelming, remember that they are all part of the past, and you are safe. These thoughts and feelings can't hurt you. But remember that trying to fight these thoughts or force yourself not to think about them can have the opposite effect: intensify them. A good exercise is to set aside a certain amount of time (no more than 15 minutes) to think about them in this non-judgmental way and then go about your day. (6)

These strategies will help you navigate your longing for the old toxic relationship during your breakup and

204 | LISANNE MURPHY

healing journey, but what if your ex is trying to win you back? How can you stop thinking about them when they try to convince you to get back together? Fortunately, we have valuable tips to help you in this scenario.

BREAKING THE CYCLE - FALLING BACK INTO A TOXIC RELATIONSHIP

Narcissists live and breathe by their ego, fed by the constant emotional abuse they inflict on their partners to feel more powerful in their toxic relationships. Their fragile ego shatters when their partner leaves them, so they will likely use manipulative tactics to win you back. Then, of course, they will say it's because they love you and want to change to make the relationship work. But remember that it's most likely about regaining control over you to maintain the image of greatness they have of themselves.

It takes an average of seven tries before someone leaves an abusive partner for good. This is not to encourage or celebrate your longing for your toxic ex but to help you be compassionate with yourself as you try your best to move on from your past relationship. (8)

If you fall back into a toxic relationship, the following strategies will help you regain your footing and commit to keeping your self-esteem at the forefront of your actions.

- **Reframe your perspective on loss and how you handle it:** As we explained in Step 1, the grieving process after breaking up with your toxic partner is likely painful because it triggers difficult emotions. This process may make you think that getting back together with your ex is better than going through the pain of heartbreak. But remember that accepting the pain with patience and compassion is how to heal. Don't rush the process; trust that there is a light at the end of the tunnel.

- **Cut all ties:** Step 5 of recovery is to set firm boundaries for yourself. If you've fallen back into the relationship, cutting off all ties may be the only option to create the space needed to be strong enough not to relapse into toxicity. Blocking your ex from social media and your phone is an excellent support strategy. When Lily cleared her life of Jack's presence and memories, she could see why being without him was much healthier.

- **Release your savior ideas:** You cannot fix or change other people. So instead of trying to save your ex-partner by "loving them enough," focus on Step 3, which is to reclaim your identity. Spend more time with yourself and work on becoming a happier, better version of yourself.

- **Build up your confidence and self-worth:** Step 2 in recovery is cultivating self-love and seeing yourself with more compassionate eyes. By celebrating your strengths and efforts and loving yourself without expecting perfection, you will naturally feel better alone than in the company of someone who doesn't truly love and value you.

- **Acknowledge and embrace what you truly deserve:** If you fall back into a toxic relationship, you must radically accept that you still deserve to be loved, fulfilled, and happy. Once you get this fact, commit to moving forward, not backward. Be aware of your inner dialogue and let go of the automatic thoughts when your ex tries to win you back, such as "This is all I'm worth" or "No one will ever love me as he did." Instead, replace them with, "I'm not going to settle for this. I deserve more." (2)

As you can see, working the 5 Steps as a cycle helps you to keep moving forward in your healing journey, even when you fall back into toxicity. You can embrace the pain instead of feeling safer returning to your "discomfort zone."

You can do this by practicing self-love and forgiving yourself for your mistakes, laying the foundation for stronger self-esteem and a more solid sense of identity. At the same time, seeking support and help from loved ones and a therapist can increase your self-awareness and encourage you to set firm boundaries to protect your happiness and well-being.

Keep working on the steps until you can relax and breathe again, even if you fall back into an unhealthy relationship. Let's not forget that awareness is a cumulative and compounding process, where each layer builds upon the previous one.

Just as peeling back the layers of an onion reveals more and more of its inner core, becoming more self-aware involves peeling back the layers of our thoughts, emotions, and behaviors to gain deeper insights into creating a comfortable life for our true selves.

Our experiences are constantly shaping our awareness, and each new layer we uncover offers new insights and opportunities for growth. But, of course, this means our awareness develops through trial and error, and yes, the "error" part is unavoidable.

The good news is that as we become more self-aware, we can make more intentional choices and take actions aligned with our values and authentic selves, leading to healthier and more fulfilling relationships. (7)

Missing your ex is normal after a breakup, and there is no specific time we can set for it to stop. However, you can take action by relying on the 5 Steps and not get sucked back into a toxic relationship.

As you stop justifying and rationalizing your partner's abusive behavior and re-educate yourself about healthy relationship dynamics, you'll be able to stop thinking about "the good old days" with your ex-partner and see things for what they were: TOXIC.

This realization will inspire you to work on your self-esteem and set goals to become your best self. Feeling the pain of mourning the relationship is never as complicated as getting back with someone whose only interest is to rob you of your identity, well-being, and potential for fulfillment. Once you work on each step of the cycle, you'll be ready to welcome healthy relationships in your life.

MAKE IT STICK

Instructions: Take some time to reflect on the following questions and answers to help you realize that it doesn't hurt to separate yourself emotionally from your ex, reevaluate what you like in a partner, and know when you're ready for a new relationship.

- **Detaching from your ex**

Activity 1: Questions To Help You Understand The Attachment To Your Ex

How can you avoid being affected by your ex's actions or words? *Use the space provided to write down strategies to avoid being bothered by your ex. For example, get off social media, avoid places where you might "accidentally" run into them, etc.*

_____

_____

_____

_____

_____

How do you stay calm when you see your ex? *Use the space provided to write down strategies such as not revealing information about your personal life, acting confident, keeping conversations short, etc.*

_____

_____

_____

_____

_____

How can you mentally and emotionally detach from your ex? *Use the space provided to write down strategies such as meditation, journaling, being patient with yourself, etc.*

_____

_____

_____

_____

_____

- **Reassessing What You Like in a Partner and Knowing When You're Ready for a New Relationship**

Activity 2: Questions About Your Choice in a Partner

Do you repeatedly make the same mistakes in choosing partners, such as selecting disrespectful, distant, or abusive partners? *Use the space provided to expound your answer.*

_____

_____

_____

_____

_____

What are the clearly defined qualities, values, and characteristics you want in a partner? Conversely, are you looking for qualities in a partner that you lack? *Use the space provided to expound your answer.*

_____

_____

_____

_____

_____

Do you focus more on whether your partner is right for you or if you are right for them? *Use the space provided to expound your answer.*

_____

_____

_____

_____

_____

Have you accepted that you cannot change another person and that they must be responsible for themselves? *Use the space provided to expound your answer.*

_____

_____

_____

_____

_____

Activity 3: Questions to Ask Yourself to Assess Your Readiness for a New Relationship

Do you have a strong sense of self and identity? Do you derive your sense of self from the people you date? *Use the space provided to expound your answer.*

Do you understand what constitutes an emotionally intelligent relationship? *Use the space provided to expound your answer.*

Do you know how to be a healthy and emotionally intelligent partner to someone? *Use the space provided to expound your answer.*

_____

_____

_____

_____

_____

Do you have fulfilling and rewarding activities outside of your dating life, or do you spend all your time with your partner? *Use the space provided to expound your answer.*

_____

_____

_____

_____

_____

Remember that missing your ex and remembering the good times is normal. It may take a while to move on to a new and fulfilling relationship. So take as much time as you need to heal and allow yourself to start your life over with a renewed sense of purpose and understanding of your wants and needs.

CONCLUSION

> *"Perhaps the butterfly is proof that you can go through a great deal of darkness yet become something beautiful."*

> — BEAU TAPLIN

As we come to the end of this book, it's important to reflect on the journey we've taken together. From understanding the complexities of toxic relationships to learning strategies to avoid falling back into them, we've explored the 5 Steps to Healing and Recovery after Leaving a Narcissistic and Emotionally Abusive Partner.

But this healing journey isn't just about following steps; it's about finding the courage to rebuild our identities after feeling like they've been shattered and feel we can't walk alone. This process will help you discover that a strong sense of self and a life of value is always possible. However, the ongoing abuse you suffered in your toxic relationship blocked your true potential and the best version of yourself.

Working through the 5 Steps to Healing and Recovery is a means to help you realize you deserve to be treated with respect, kindness, and love–from others and yourself. And the importance of taking action to create a fulfilling life.

Realizing we have been in a toxic relationship is the first and most painful reality check after the relationship ends. After all, narcissistic partners know exactly how to keep you under their spell and trick you into believing that the hell you are living is true love, happiness, and the best you can get.

But accepting that you share some responsibility for ending up in a toxic relationship is heartbreaking and often difficult to accept. But it isn't about feeling guilty or ashamed; this realization opens the door to the 5 Steps to Healing: allowing yourself to feel the pain, strengthening the inner self through forgiveness and self-love, seeking professional help, reclaiming your identity, and setting boundaries to rebuild your world.

Healing and recovering from toxic relationships is a confusing and sometimes bewildering process that takes time, patience, and commitment. The 5 Steps are not linear; expecting them to be linear can make things seem more problematic than needed. Instead, the more you embrace the journey and walk through it without fighting or cursing your luck, the more rewarding and exciting you will discover it to be.

As you open your heart and mind to the pain that inevitably comes with grief, you'll learn to forgive yourself and rediscover your interests and activities that bring you joy and pleasure. Asking for help also opens you up to a world of people who have been through the same experience and are eager to guide and support you as you rebuild your identity.

Sometimes setting boundaries comes naturally, and sometimes you must work hard to stick to them to avoid getting hurt again. One day you'll feel confident and eager to meet new people; other days, you'll wake up with memories of your ex stuck in your head. It's all part of the process. Acknowledge your successes and efforts, no matter how small they seem, and set small but manageable goals that can move you closer to living in alignment with your authentic self.

After hearing about Lily's initial breakup with Jack, we met for lunch every few weeks. It was amazing to watch her healing transformation. In the meantime, I researched, talked to other friends and colleagues, and came to an enlightening and encouraging conclusion. Lily's healing experience was not unique to her. These steps in the cycle are the common denominator used by anyone trying to heal from a toxic relationship.

At the end of one of our lunches, I hugged and thanked her for sharing her story. Lily just smiled and replied that she's learned from experience that sharing her story cultivates empathy, compassion, and vulnerability for all involved. As a result, others feel more comfortable sharing their own harrowing stories. And it gives Lily a sense of meaning and purpose for her own suffering.

Then her phone rang. It was her new boyfriend, Liam, who was proving daily to be a healthy, fulfilling, and rewarding partner.

On her way out to meet Liam, I asked, "Was it hard to trust again?" Without missing a beat, she quickly replied that trusting again was the easiest, most natural decision because of her healing journey.

Use this book as a manual to equip yourself with the steps to recover from narcissistic abuse and toxic relationships. Return to each step as you need them to help yourself on the healing journey to breathe again.

Oh, for those of you wanting additional support for the toxic relationships you may be encountering outside of romantic partnerships, this bit is for you. Toxic relationships can occur in any context: romantic, professional, friends, or family. While most of this book focuses on toxic romantic relationships, the principles and lessons gained apply to all unhealthy relationships.

As a special bonus, exclusively for readers of this book, there is an additional BONUS chapter that delves deeper into how to navigate toxic relationships at work and among family and friends. Go to www.healingtoxicity.com/breathe-again-bonus for access to this free Ebook.

One last thing, with all the valuable knowledge to help you heal and overcome toxic relationships right here, it's time to share your experience and show other readers where they can find the same help.

By leaving your honest review of this book on Amazon, you'll show others struggling in toxic relationships where to find the information they're looking for to continue their healing journey and pass on their newfound strength to others who may need it.

Thank you for your help. The cycle of toxic relationships can be broken if we share our knowledge and support each other - by leaving a review, you're helping me do just that.

Scan the QR code for a quick review!

REFERENCES

REFERENCES CHAPTER 1: UNRAVELING THE COMPLEXITIES OF A TOXIC RELATIONSHIP

Ambardar, Sheenie (2021, July 1). Narcissistic Personality Disorder. Retrieved March 15, 2023, from https://emedicine.medscape.com/article/1519417-overview#a5 **(3)**

Bame, Y. (2017) *3 in 4 US adults don't know what gaslighting is, YouGov.* Available at: https://today.yougov.com/topics/health/articles-reports/2017/06/27/it-could-be-happening-you-3-4-us-adults-dont-know- (Accessed: March 24, 2023). **(5)**

How gaslighting and narcissism are related (no date) *ReGain.* Available at: https://www.regain.us/advice/general/how-gaslighting-and-narcissism-are-related/ (Accessed: March 15, 2023). **(6)**

Huizem Jennifer.(no date) *What is gaslighting? examples and how to respond. Medical News Today.* MediLexicon International. Available at: https://www.medicalnewstoday.com/articles/gaslighting#how-it-works (Accessed: March 16, 2023). **(4)**

Melinda Smith, M. A. (2023, March 1). Narcissistic personality disorder. HelpGuide.org. Retrieved March 15, 2023, from https://www.helpguide.org/articles/mental-disorders/narcissistic-personality-disorder.htm **(2)**

Scott, E. [2022/11/04]. *What Is a Toxic Relationship? Verywell Mind.* Retrieved March 14, 2023, from https://www.verywellmind.com/toxic-relationships-4174665 **(1)**

Sussex Publishers. (n.d.). *The effects of narcissistic supply in a toxic relationship.* Psychology Today. Retrieved March 15, 2023, Retrieved March 14, 2023, from https://www.psychologytoday.com/us/blog/addiction-and-recovery/202106/the-effects-narcissistic-supply-in-toxic-relationship **(2)**

REFERENCES CHAPTER 2: HOW DID I GET HERE? UNDERSTANDING YOUR ROLE IN A TOXIC RELATIONSHIP

Bijan Kholghi (2023) *11 reasons: "why do I attract toxic people?" & how to change, Coaching Online.* Available at: https://www.coaching-online. org/why-do-i-attract-toxic-people/ (Accessed: March 22, 2023). **(1)**

Emotional dependency - toxic relationships and why it's so hard to let ... (no date). Available at: https://www.joinresilio.com/post/emotional-dependency-toxic-relationships-and-why-it-s-so-hard-to-let-them-go (Accessed: March 28, 2023). **(2)**

Early family experience affects later romantic relationships (2018) *National Institutes of Health.* U.S. Department of Health and Human Services. Available at: https://www.nih.gov/news-events/nih-research-matters/early-family-experience-affects-later-romantic-relation ships (Accessed: March 24, 2023). **(6)**

Gould, W.R. (2022) *What is codependency?, Verywell Mind.* Verywell Mind. Available at: https://www.verywellmind.com/what-is-code pendency-5072124 (Accessed: March 24, 2023). **(5)**

Hurd, S. (2022) *6 psychological reasons you attract toxic relationships, Learning Mind.* Available at: https://www.learning-mind.com/ attract-toxic-relationships/ (Accessed: March 23, 2023). **(3)**

Jacobsen, J. (2022) How to heal core wounds for better relationships, Marriage Advice - Expert Marriage Tips & Advice. Available at: https://www.marriage.com/advice/mental-health/healing-core-wounds/#What_are_the_core_wounds (Accessed: March 24, 2023). **(7)**

Studies show people with low self-esteem unintentionally encourage ... (no date). Available at: https://www.inc.com/amy-morin/studies-show-people-with-low-self-esteem-unintentionally-encourage-people-to-treat-them-poorly.html (Accessed: March 22, 2023). **(4)**

Understanding your core wound and false self (no date) *Shelley Klammer.* Available at: https://intuitivecreativity.typepad.com/expres

siveartinspirations/2014/07/understanding-your-core-pain-and-false-self.html (Accessed: March 27, 2023). **(8)**

REFERENCES CHAPTER 3: EMBRACING THE END: CREATING CLOSURE IN TOXIC RELATIONSHIPS

Bockarova, M. (no date) *Why we need closure from broken relationships, Psychology Today*. Sussex Publishers. Available at: https://www.psychologytoday.com/us/blog/romantically-attached/201609/why-we-need-closure-broken-relationships (Accessed: March 28, 2023). **(4)**

Catalog, T. (2021b, December 12). The Real Reasons Your Toxic Ex Keeps Crawling Back — According To Research. Medium. https://thoughtcatalog.medium.com/the-real-reasons-your-toxic-ex-keeps-crawling-back-according-to-research-3e79705be2d **(8)**

Fisher, H. L., Xu, X., Aron, A., & Brown, L. L. (2016, May 10). Intense, Passionate, Romantic Love: A Natural Addiction? How the Fields That Investigate Romance and Substance Abuse Can Inform Each Other. Frontiers in Psychology; Frontiers Media. https://doi.org/10.3389/fpsyg.2016.00687 **(10)**

Gould, W.R. (2022) *What is closure in a relationship?, Verywell Mind*. Verywell Mind. Available at: https://www.verywellmind.com/what-is-closure-in-a-relationship-5224411 (Accessed: March 28, 2023). **(5)**

Psychreg (2022) *5 ways narcissistic abuse affects your body and mind, Psychreg*. Available at: https://www.psychreg.org/narcissistic-abuse-affects-body-mind/ (Accessed: March 27, 2023). **(3)**

Testa, G. (2023, February 6). How To Give Yourself Closure After A Breakup. Bolde. https://www.bolde.com/10-ways-give-yourself-closure-breakup/ **(7)**

journal of positive psychology. (n.d.). The Economic Times. https://economictimes.indiatimes.com/topic/journal-of-positive-psychology **(6)**

The Healthy Journal - Gluten, Dairy, Sugar Free Recipes, Interviews and Health Articles. (n.d.). https://www.thehealthyjournal.com. https://thehealthyjournal.com/q-and-a/why-do-toxic-exes-come-back (9)

Wedia (2020) *Why is it so hard to leave a toxic relationship?, IamExpat.* Available at: https://www.iamexpat.nl/lifestyle/lifestyle-news/why-it-so-hard-leave-toxic-relationship%E2%80%8B (Accessed: March 27, 2023). (2)

Young, K. (2020) *When someone you love is toxic - how to let go, without guilt, Hey Sigmund.* Available at: https://www.heysigmund.com/toxic-people-when-someone-you-love-toxic/ (Accessed: March 27, 2023). (1)

REFERENCES CHAPTER 4: STEP 1: ALLOWING YOURSELF TO FEEL THE PAIN

Bueso-Izquierdo, N., Guerrero-Molina, M., Verdejo-Román, J., & Moreno-Manso, J. M. (2022, January 1). The three faces of intimate partner violence against women seen from the neuroimaging studies: A literature review. Aggression and Violent Behavior; Elsevier BV. https://doi.org/10.1016/j.avb.2022.101720 (3)

Gillies, Kaytee. (2023, February 20). Choosing Therapy. Emotional Hangovers: Definition, Causes, & How to Cope. Choosing Therapy.https://www.choosingtherapy.com/emotional-hangover/ (1)

How grief affects your brain and what to do about it. (2019, August 13). NBC News. https://www.nbcnews.com/better/lifestyle/how-mourn-breakup-so-you-can-truly-move-ncna1034181 (6)

Jacobsen, J., & Jacobsen, J. (2022, July 7). 7 Stages of Healing & Recovery After Narcissistic Abuse. Marriage Advice - Expert Marriage Tips & Advice. https://www.marriage.com/advice/mental-health/stages-of-healing-after-narcissistic-abuse/#What_happens_to_your_brain_after_narcissistic_abuse (4)

Maertz, Kim (date unknown). https://uca.edu/counseling/files/ 2012/09/Surviving-A-Relationship-Break-1.pdf (7)

Tech, S. (2023, January 14). The Emotional Hangover from Leaving a Narcissistic Relationship by Roberta Cone, Psy.D. Straight Talk Clinic. https://www.straighttalkcounseling.org/post/the-emotional-hangover-from-leaving-a-narcissistic-relationship-by-roberta-cone-psy-d (2)

REFERENCES CHAPTER 5: STEP 2: STRENGTHENING THE INNER SELF THROUGH FORGIVENESS AND SELF-LOVE

Crady, A. (2022b, January 6). 12 Powerful Ways to Love Yourself After Narcissistic Abuse. Medium. https://medium.com/the-virago/12-powerful-ways-to-love-yourself-after-narcissistic-abuse-450e83fc7c3 (5)

Davis, S. (2021, January 25). Overcoming Emotional Flashbacks with Self-Compassion | CPTSDfoundation.org. https://cptsdfoundation. org/2021/01/25/overcoming-emotional-flashbacks-with-self-compassion/ (3)

Evans, M. T. (2016, September 19). Forgiving Yourself For Being Hooked and Tricked By The Narcissist. Narcissism Recovery and Relationships Blog. https://blog.melanietoniaevans.com/forgiving-yourself-for-being-hooked-and-tricked-by-the-narcissist/ (2)

Forgiving Yourself After Narcissistic Abuse. (n.d.). Psychopath Free. https://www.psychopathfree.com/articles/forgiving-yourself-after-narcissistic-abuse.366/ (1)

Naim, R. (2021, August 26). Self-Love Is The Best Form Of Healing. Thought Catalog. https://thoughtcatalog.com/rania-naim/2019/ 04/self-love-is-the-best-form-of-healing/ (4)

REFERENCES CHAPTER 6: STEP 3 - SEEKING SUPPORT FROM PROFESSIONALS IN HEALING

Eatough, Erin (2021). Seeking Help for Your Mental Health Is Brave. And Beneficial. https://www.betterup.com/blog/seeking-help (1)

Massicotte, P. G. (2021, February 25). Why Is It So Hard To Ask For Help When Facing Psychological Distress? — Beautiful Voyager. Beautiful Voyager. https://bevoya.com/blog/hard-for-men-to-ask-for-help-mental-health (3)

Mueller, S. (2020, February 1). 60 awesome baseball quotes. Planet of Success. https://www.planetofsuccess.com/blog/2017/baseball-quotes/ (6)

Oladipo, G. (2021, June 21). How To Find the Right Therapist: 10 Tips. Psych Central. https://psychcentral.com/blog/10-ways-to-find-a-good-therapist#what-to-avoid (5)

Peterson, Tanya (2020). 4 Reasons Why It's Okay to Seek Mental Health Help | HealthyPlace. (2020, June 22). https://www.healthyplace.com/other-info/mental-health-newsletter/4-reasons-why-its-okay-to-seek-mental-health-help (2)

Smith, M., MA. (2023, February 22). Finding a Therapist Who Can Help You Heal. HelpGuide.org. https://www.helpguide.org/articles/mental-health/finding-a-therapist-who-can-help-you-heal.htm (4)

Snapper, E. (2016, June 27). Charitable MLB players. Fanatics Forum. https://blog.fanatics.com/giving-back-mlb/ (6)

REFERENCES CHAPTER 7: STEP 4: RECLAIMING YOUR IDENTITY IN THE AFTERMATH OF A TOXIC RELATIONSHIP

Allan, D. G. (2018, March 1). Ben Franklin's '13 Virtues' path to personal perfection. CNN. https://edition.cnn.com/2018/03/01/health/13-virtues-wisdom-project/index.html (7)

Boundless. (2018, October 4). 10 Things That Don't Define You - Boundless. https://www.boundless.org/blog/10-things-that-dont-define-you/ **(1)**

Educator, K. S.-. A. R. (2018, August 22). Healing from Identity Loss After Narcissistic Abuse. Psych Central. https://psychcentral.com/blog/liberation/2018/08/healing-from-identity-loss-after-narcissis tic-abuse#Healing-Identity-Loss-Is-an-Ongoing-Process **(3)**

Gordon, S. (2023, March 6). 8 Ways to Feel Better After a Breakup. Verywell Mind. https://www.verywellmind.com/8-ways-to-feel-better-after-a-breakup-5089116 **(4)**

How Self-Compassion Can Help You Through a Breakup. (n.d.). Greater Good. https://greatergood.berkeley.edu/article/item/how_self_compassion_can_help_you_through_divorce **(5)**

MindTools | Home. (n.d.). https://www.mindtools.com/a4wo118/smart-goals **(8)**

Perera BA, MA, DipLC, K., & DipLC, K. P. B. M. (2022, February 8). Self Awareness and Self Esteem. More Self Esteem. https://more-selfesteem.com/more-self-esteem/building-self-esteem/what-is-self-esteem/self-awareness-and-self-esteem/ **(6)**

Saeed, K. (2020, October 30). Loss of Identity: Examples of Perspecticide from Narcissistic Abuse. Kim Saeed. https://kimsaeed.com/2018/08/15/loss-of-identity-examples-of-perspecti cide-from-narcissistic-abuse/ **(2)**

REFERENCES CHAPTER 8: STEP 5: BOUNDARIES - THE KEY TO REBUILDING YOUR WORLD

Jancar, M. (2023). The Guide To Setting Healthy Boundaries With Your Ex. Max Jancar. https://maxjancar.com/setting-boundaries-with-an-ex/ **(4)**

Lcsw, S. M. (2020, April 30). How to Set Boundaries with Toxic People. Psych Central. https://psychcentral.com/blog/imperfect/2020/04/how-to-set-boundaries-with-toxic-people **(3)**

Manson, M. (2023, February 8). The Guide to Strong Relationship Boundaries. Mark Manson. https://markmanson.net/boundaries (2)

PsyD, K. D. (2023). 5 Ways To Stop Having the Same Kind of Unhealthy Relationship — Kristin Davin, Psy.D., Clinical Psychologist. Kristin Davin, Psy.D., Clinical Psychologist. https://reflectionsfromacrossthecouch.com/blog/5-ways-to-stop-having-the-same-kind-of-unhealthy-relationship (6)

Theriault, C. (2022). How to Shut Down a Toxic Person and Establish Your Boundaries. Motherhood + Mayhem. https://motherhoodandmayhem.online/shut-down-toxic-ex-boundaries/ (5)

Zola, M. (2021, August 12). How to Set Healthy Boundaries in Your Relationship. Eugene Therapy. https://eugenetherapy.com/article/how-to-set-healthy-boundaries-in-your-relationship/ (1)

REFERENCES CHAPTER 9: THE 5 STEPS IN ACTION: A COMPREHENSIVE FRAMEWORK FOR HEALING

Gutierrez, G. (2022, January 30). Setting Boundaries with an Ex- Is it Still Possible? - Harness Magazine. Harness Magazine. https://www.harnessmagazine.com/setting-boundaries-with-an-ex/ (4)

Kvalentine. (2021, October 28). Self Awareness And Grieving - Bakken Young Funeral Home - River Falls and New Richmond Wi. Bakken Young Funeral Home - River Falls and New Richmond Wi. https://bakken-young.com/self-awareness-and-grieving/ (5)

Raypole, Crystal (2020, June 18) 'Who Am I?' How to Find Your Sense of Self. Healthline. https://www.healthline.com/health/sense-of-self#finding-support%5C (2)

Smith, M., MA. (2023b). Coping with a Breakup or Divorce. HelpGuide.org. https://www.helpguide.org/articles/grief/dealing-with-a-breakup-or-divorce.htm (3)

Shockley, S. A., & Shockley, S. A. (2018). 7 Ways To Love Yourself

Through Chronic Pain. Soul Analyse. https://soulanalyse.com/blog/7-ways-to-love-yourself-through-chronic-pain/ **(1)**

REFERENCES CHAPTER 10: STAYING ON TRACK: HOW TO HANDLE RELAPSE IN A TOXIC RELATIONSHIP

Akin, E. (2023, April 14). How Do I Stop Thinking About My Narcissistic Ex? - Unfilteredd. Unfilteredd. https://unfilteredd.net/how-do-i-stop-thinking-about-my-narcissistic-ex/ **(5)**

Gupta, S. (2020, December 1). 6 reasons why getting back together with your ex is a truly terrible idea. Healthshots. https://www.healthshots.com/mind/emotional-health/6-reasons-why-getting-back-together-with-your-ex-is-a-truly-terrible-idea/ **(4)**

Gupta, A. (2021, October 8). Why do I keep going back to a toxic relationship? Hope Heals Therapy. https://www.hopehealstherapy.com/why-do-i-keep-going-back-to-a-toxic-relationship/ **(1)**

Johnson, E. (2021, December 14). Why you keep going back to toxic relationships | Practical Growth. Medium. https://medium.com/practical-growth/why-you-keep-going-back-to-toxic-relationships-94d7e3a1d55b **(2)**

Nguyen, E. (2022, January 5). 5 Ways to Stop Reminiscing about the Good Times with a Toxic Ex. Medium. https://medium.com/love fulmind/5-ways-to-stop-reminiscing-about-the-good-times-with-a-toxic-ex-476a638c1ee **(6)**

Nik. (2022, May 18). How to *Really* Develop Self-Awareness - nik.art. nik.art. https://nik.art/how-to-develop-self-awareness/ **(7)**

Unhealthy Relationships. (n.d.-b). Planned Parenthood. https://www.plannedparenthood.org/learn/relationships/healthy-relationships/what-makes-relationship-unhealthy **(3)**

Planned Parenthood. (n.d.). https://www.plannedparenthood.org/learn/relationships/healthy-relationships/what-makes-relation ship-unhealthy **(8)**